THE
TWELFTH CENTURY
RENAISSANCE

THE TWELFTH CENTURY RENAISSANCE

CHRISTOPHER BROOKE

with 132 illustrations, 21 in colour

THAMES AND HUDSON · LONDON

FOR JOAN EVANS

© COPYRIGHT 1969 CHRISTOPHER BROOKE

PRINTED IN GREAT BRITAIN BY JARROLD AND SONS LTD NORWICH

500 32017 9 CLOTHBOUND

500 33017 4 PAPERBOUND

CONTENTS

This book aims to give an insight into the cultural movements of the twelfth century by combining copious pictures and quotations with an attempt to interpret them. Interpretation there must be, so long as it opens windows into the twelfth century and does not act as a screen, keeping the reader from direct entry into that world. The book surveys its field topic by topic – schools, learning and theology; Latin literature, letters and humanism; canon law and the organization of the Church; architecture and art; vernacular literature and its links with Latin culture and the schools. Each of these topics is built round the careers of one or more central figures of the renaissance, Abelard, John of Salisbury, Master Gratian, Gilbert the sculptor, and so forth; the prologue sets the stage, and considers the questions to be asked, and the achievement of some of the earlier books on the subject; the epilogue defines to what extent the renaissance had an ending, to what extent it was continued in the centuries which followed. It is rash to write a small book on a great theme; my excuse is that the text is aimed to help the reader, through the pictures and the notes on books, to pursue the renaissance for himself.

I owe many debts. First to Professor Geoffrey Barraclough, the General Editor, to Mr Stanley Baron of Messrs Thames and Hudson, and to my wife, Dr Rosalind Brooke, for much encouragement and penetrating criticism: from this the book has greatly benefited; if I had been able to meet all their criticisms, its shortcomings would be much the fewer. With great generosity Dr Marianne Wynn read the sections on vernacular (and especially German) literature, Professor George Zarnecki the chapter on art and architecture. They eradicated many errors; some, no doubt, still remain, but they are all my

7

own. With Mrs G. Bruckner and Miss R. Rosenberg of Messrs Thames and Hudson I have had a happy collaboration on the plates. Many others have helped; my youngest son, Patrick, has given much help with the index, and a number of audiences have patiently borne lectures based on themes of chapters of this book, to its advantage, if not to theirs. Mr Hugh Sacker first revealed to me the riches of German literature in this period; to many aspects of the twelfth century, from the letters of St Bernard to the writings of Emile Mâle, I was introduced by Professor Dom David Knowles; and it was my father who brought me up to know the special delight of studying the twelfth century.

Westfield College,
University of London   *February 1969*

THE PROBLEM OF THE TWELFTH CENTURY RENAISSANCE:
THE QUESTIONS POSED

If an answer had to be given to the question, who has been the most influential historian of the twelfth century? – a very strong case could be made for Geoffrey of Monmouth, author of the *History of the Kings of Britain*, which was completed in or about 1138. At a point in his narrative which may be placed approximately in the fourth century BC, Geoffrey tells us that the dynasty of King Lear finally came to an end, and 'courage roused a young man named Dunuallo Molmutius' to reunite the kingdom of Britain under his sway. 'This prince set up the laws the Britons call the Molmutine laws, which are held in honour among the English till this day. In these, among other items described by St Gildas long years after, he laid down that the temples of the gods . . . should have the privilege of sanctuary . . .; likewise the roads leading to the temples . . . and the ploughs of husbandmen . . . At last, after a reign of forty years spent in these and other acts of government, he died, and was buried in the city of *Trinovantum* near the temple of Concord, which he himself built as a prop and stay to the laws. . . .' Later Geoffrey describes how Molmutius' work was continued by his son and successor Belinus, who built roads of stone and mortar the whole length of the island, and gave his roads special privileges. 'But if anyone desires to know all that he laid down as to the roads, let him read the Molmutine laws, which Gildas the historian translated from British to Latin, and King Alfred into English.'[1]

Geoffrey's book was written by a man with a shrewd eye for the remains of the past, especially of the Roman past, a wide

9

knowledge of ancient and not so ancient literature, for an audience which lived and respected the past but knew little about it. It was written in the style of serious history, and serious history it claimed to be; and for the most part it was taken at face value. Yet this account of Molmutius and his son is an impudent fiction, though every line is calculated to tickle the fancy of the *conoscente*, for Geoffrey's history is a pastiche of reminiscences of the genuine past, carefully placed in a new historical context. He succeeded, I suspect, beyond his dreams, for what appeared to be serious history, and was intended (perhaps not very seriously intended) to be read as serious history, was in fact a substantial work of fiction. Every line in it reflects the interest of twelfth century Englishmen in the past, and their respect for the past; and every line reflects an age with a wholly new capacity for imaginative fiction.

A generation later a learned clerk called William Fitz-Stephen set to work to write a life of his master, St Thomas Becket, recently martyred. William and Thomas were both born in London, and for the greatest of English cities William showed a fanatical devotion akin to that which adorned the Italian cities of the fifteenth century with the masterpieces of art and architecture of the Italian renaissance. 'Plato sketched the shape of a Republic in a discourse; Sallust described the situation of Africa in his *History* on account of the Carthaginian rebellion against the Romans . . . and I shall now describe the site and commonwealth of London on account of St Thomas.'

FitzStephen wrote in all earnestness, yet it is abundantly clear that (like all his western contemporaries) he knew nothing at first hand of Plato's *Republic*, and (unlike many twelfth century historians) he had not read Sallust, or had forgotten his works if he had. His was a world in which one can meet genuine appreciation of the past, pagan and Christian, and real sympathy and insight into classical Latin literature; but also an astonishing wealth of ignorance. It was a world in which men could enquire as to the origin of treasured institutions, and listen to Geoffrey expounding the laws of Molmutius, still well known and held in honour; could gulp as we all do when faced with our own ignorance, and say: 'The laws of Molmutius: but yes, of course.'

Not everyone, however, was deceived, and Geoffrey, the parodist, was in his turn parodied by the satirist Walter Map; and the insight men like Map evidently had into the methods of Geoffrey's fiction helps to explain the inspiration Geoffrey gave to creative writing later in the century. His greatest creation was King Arthur. Here, for once, Geoffrey based his narrative on a nucleus of fact; and before Geoffrey wrote, Arthur was the hero of Breton lays, had inspired an Italian sculptor and had children at the font named after him in several parts of Europe. But it was Geoffrey who floated King Arthur on the cosmopolitan literary world of the twelfth century as a respectable figure for other courts than those of the Welsh princes to honour, and first traced the pattern by which legend could become the base of creative fiction. A direct line leads from Geoffrey's bravado in attributing current knowledge of the Molmutine laws to Gildas and Alfred to the famous passage in Wolfram's *Parzival* in which the author takes to task the French Chrétien of Troyes (his chief source) for getting the story wrong, and claims to have put it right with the help of Kyot of Provence, 'who has offered us the true story' from the Arabic. The interest of twelfth century writers in the past, especially the classical past, can be both deeply naive and highly sophisticated; the same is equally true of the courtly romances of the late twelfth and early thirteenth centuries. It is unlikely that Wolfram knew Geoffrey at first hand. But he absorbed an extraordinary amount of the culture of his world in his poverty-stricken, knightly home in south Germany: echoes of the theological ideas of the twelfth century schools, of the literary productions of the French courts, mingle in the rich fabrics of his tales.

At the end of the day, was the civilization of twelfth century Christendom derivative or creative? In what measure was it the product of European experience, or of contact with the

Arabic world of Wolfram's fancy? Was it dominated by the Latin culture of the schools or the French culture of the court of the Angevins? In what measure did different parts of Christendom contribute to it? These are some of the questions forced on us by a brief inspection of a single sample: such are the themes of this book.

1 Arthur before Geoffrey of Monmouth; Modena cathedral, doorway, probably 1099–1120. 'Artus de Bretania' attacks a castle

It must be firmly stated at the outset that the phrase 'the twelfth century Renaissance' has no precise meaning. It carries overtones, and these are essential to understanding an exciting epoch in human history. We are still far from a full comprehension of the depths of the love of men of that age for the antique, or of the meaning of twelfth century humanism. But it is vain to search for a definition. Historians love to use labels of this kind; and in the hands of a master they can assume real meaning. Burckhardt gave real meaning – for a time – to the Renaissance of the fifteenth century; and a few historians have given real meaning even to 'feudalism'. But most discussions of these terms lapse into arid semantics, and lose contact with the actual flow of human effort and events. Observers of such a dusty Armageddon have been tempted to doubt if the movement behind the label ever existed. Yet this can surely not be put in question: however difficult to define, however elusive its 'essence', what happened in Italy in the fifteenth century was one of the great movements of the human spirit; and so, surely enough, were the movements in education, in spiritual and cultural life, thought and art of the twelfth century. In an article on the English contribution to this renaissance, R. W. Southern quietly and characteristically tidied the semantics into a cupboard by referring to the 'sublime meaninglessness' of the label.[2]

Following this lead, we may define the elements in the cultural life of the twelfth century to which it has become attached as developments in theology – in the methods of theological discussion, and systematization of theological thought; in logic and grammar; in canon law; in religious organization; in art and architecture; and in vernacular poetry. Here is a formidable syllabus for a small book. Every one of these elements must be in our minds if we are to do any sort of justice to the richness of the theme; and two other problems dictate our approach to it. The cultural movements of the twelfth century were cosmopolitan; for some of the elements the clear centre lay in France, but every part of Europe made its own contribution – even England, as it was the special purpose of Professor Southern's article to show.

It was the eighteenth century which canonized the notion of the Renaissance, and we have never quite shaken off the influence of the terms then put in vogue. The middle age between the world of Greece and Rome and its effective reassertion in the Italian Renaissance was the world of Gothic – of the triumph of barbarism and religion. In course of time, especially in the nineteenth century, careful investigation began of the origins of the Renaissance, and in a world which had come to admire Gothic, not to revile it. From this sprang all manner of confusion, but also real illumination. Thus it is illuminating to see that many aspects of the Italian Renaissance presuppose earlier movements; that the achievement of the humanists was securely based on the work of classical scholars of the ninth, eleventh and twelfth centuries; or that the dedication of Renaissance artists to the outward appearance of nature owed something to the world of ideas in which St Francis had lived at the turn of the twelfth and thirteenth centuries; or again, that in the twelfth century itself the two most notably original artistic creations were Gothic architecture and vernacular poetry, and that some link might well exist between them. But if this leads us to anticipate what was characteristic of the *Quattrocento* in the Carolingian renaissance of the eighth and ninth centuries, or in the Ottonian renaissance of the tenth and eleventh or even in the renaissance of the twelfth century, it can only lead to confusion; and it would be equally confusing to imagine St Francis in the company of the Florentine humanists, or to isolate Gothic architecture and French and German vernacular literature as unique expressions of the 'Gothic' spirit.

The themes of this book are the cultural movements of the twelfth century in western Christendom. I try to see them in unity and variety; I try to see them in relation to earlier centuries and to movements of later days; above all, to observe the links between the different elements in the story. But no attempt is made to force these movements into moulds. For all the semantics, this has happily been the tradition of most scholars who have worked in the field, even though their approach has often been eclectic. *The Renaissance of the Twelfth Century*, by the great American medievalist C. H. Haskins,[*] dwelt on the Latin culture of the age: on books and libraries, on grammar and rhetoric. Science, theology and canon law each had a share of attention, but the approach was essentially Latin and literary. Vernacular literature was no part of his theme; nor were art and architecture. In the forty years since Haskins wrote, every aspect of the subject has enjoyed its own renaissance. The vast literature on schools and scholarship, on law and theology, is well represented in the standard text-book of Paré, Brunet and Tremblay, *La renaissance du douzième siècle*, in which notable justice is paid both to the personal contribution of great teachers like Abelard and to the growing formalism and system in study which led to the formation of universities. In contrast, one might almost suppose at first reading that the portions of Erwin Panofsky's *Renaissance and Renascence* which concern the twelfth century described a different epoch or a different planet; although one cannot accuse the author of that brilliant extravaganza *Art and Scholasticism* of indifference to the theological studies of the schools. Panofsky distinguishes two movements in this age. First, a movement with its base in Italy and southern France which delighted in the direct copying of antique works of art. Thus the famous equestrian statue of Marcus Aurelius in Rome was identified with Constantine, and this imagined image of the first Christian emperor was multiplied many times in western Europe, and even spread as far north as Herefordshire. But this was a movement of imitation not normally involving real sympathy or understanding. From

[*] All the books referred to are listed on pp. 203–7.

COPYING OF ANTIQUE WORKS

The statue of Marcus Aurelius in Rome, which was thought to be a statue of Constantine, was the ultimate model for many medieval equestrian reliefs and paintings, especially in the twelfth century, of Constantine and St George

2 Constantine the Great at Parthenay-le-Vieux; tympanum of the church of St Hilaire

3 Constantine at Poitiers; eleventh–twelfth century wall-painting in the Baptistery

4 Marcus Aurelius; Rome, Capitol

5 St George and the Dragon, tympanum at Brinsop (Herefordshire)

the north, Panofsky argued, came the second, literary movement showing a real penetration of the antique, whose special character was humanism – a humanism anticipating in many respects that of the later Renaissance, both in its love of ancient literature and in its concern with human values and personality.

The wider setting of our story is brilliantly described in R. W. Southern's *Making of the Middle Ages*, in which the values and interest which are our theme are painted as a silent revolution, which came like a thief in the night. 'This silence in the great changes of history is something which meets us everywhere as we go through' the centuries from the late tenth to the early thirteenth. Yet 'the secret revolution of these centuries did not pass unnoticed by contemporaries. By the second half of the twelfth century, the consciousness of new achievement was widespread, especially among those who practised the art of poetry. The form in which the new historical perspective expressed itself was as a movement of "chivalry and learning" – all that we comprehend in the word "civilization" – from Greece to Rome, and from Rome after a long interval to France, the mainstay of western Christendom.'[3] This put the problem of describing such a movement in a nutshell: it was in its depth like all such movements, silent and unobserved; we must relate its social background, its sources and origins, in so far as we can by glancing at the roots and runners beneath the soil. But it was not wholly unobserved: it rejoiced in its own achievement. The twelfth century renaissance is unthinkable without the creative teachers, writers and artists which made its cultural achievement of lasting value and interest; and to these too we must do justice.

Hence the theme of this book is the relation of a few selected, creative men and women to the world in which they were born, with its extraordinary limitations and opportunities.

18

RELIGIOUS SENTIMENT IN THE TWELFTH CENTURY

The twelfth century lay in the centre of the ages of faith, and it is commonly assumed that the key to its understanding lies in theology. Were not all men believers and all their achievements coloured by their faith? Was not the *Geist*, the spirit of the age, peculiarly Christian and Catholic? There is a sense in which one must say yes to these questions; but not too easily. Let us observe in passing that the *succès fou* of heresies, especially in southern France and Italy, was one of the striking facts of twelfth century history; and pass on to ask this question of the most notable witnesses we have of the range of human concern and human interest among ordinary folk of the period about 1200: the three large vernacular epics written in German about the turn of the century or shortly after, the *Nibelungenlied*, Wolfram's *Parzival* and the *Tristan* of Gottfried von Strassburg. Before Dante, they mark the summit of medieval literature; so it is a little like asking the Elizabethan dramatists to tell us what ordinary folk thought in the sixteenth century. Their authors were not men of a common mould; but they have this peculiar advantage, that they had the art and the will to show us a range of interest and ideas, in a vivid and perceptible form, which makes them – imaginatively and discreetly used – far better guides to the sentiment of their age than its formal theology.

The *Nibelungenlied* and the *Parzival* both inspired great works by Wagner, and both represent the tastes of German layfolk of their age; otherwise they are profoundly different. The author of the *Nibelungenlied* betrays no interest in religion at all, and if one reads his poem without *parti pris*, one would

19

take it that theological issues, religious issues of any kind, were not of any concern to him. The *Parzival* is the work of an uneducated knight, proud of his status: it lacks all the trappings of the ecclesiastical world, and it seems that the Grail has been turned from a cup to a stone to avoid any confusion with a chalice. Yet Wolfram was a deeply religious man; a Christian criticism of the world of 'chivalry' is near the heart of his purpose, and there is much in this poem – more yet in his other great epic, the *Willehalm* – which presupposes the theological movements of the twelfth century. Near the heart of his purpose: yet nearer still is an exploration of doubt and despair, so searching as to make clear that these were qualities perfectly familiar in Wolfram's world, that 'simple faith' was no universal quality. Gottfried's *Tristan* wears on its sleeve the influence of the twelfth century schools: it is far the most sophisticated of the three. Whatever its purpose, the effect it makes on a reader embarking on it with a fairly open mind is that the view of courtly love★ as a parody of religious faith has been deliberately, ironically and horrifyingly drawn out at every stage. The Cave of Lovers in which Tristan and Isolde faithfully obey love's precepts is described as if it were a church, richly adorned, with a saint's shrine – 'the bed of crystalline Love' – in its centre; and its proportions and design are symbolically

★ Like most historical labels, the phrase is variously used, and can cause confusion (see p. 175). In its narrowest, strictest sense, it describes a strict set of principles, first found in western Europe in the Provençal lyric of the eleventh century. The good knight, who wishes to be recognized at court as a model of courtesy, declares himself the slave of a lady who is commonly unattainable and always capricious; and he bases his conduct on her whims and the dictates of the god of Love. This artificial, literary sentiment became in the twelfth century a part of a much wider, more diverse sentiment which is the origin of the western tradition of romantic love and courtesy. To make clear-cut distinctions between different aspects of the religion of human Love can be very misleading; and to call the sentiment in its broader sense 'romantic love' obscures for a modern reader the sharp edges and acute human insight which were often revealed by medieval poets. For these reasons, courtly love is commonly used in this book in a fairly wide sense, for all types of human love in which (in contemporary eyes) there was an element of religious cult – the cult of Love, of Cupid – or in which there was some relation between love, courtesy and the subjection of man to woman, in a manner contrary to the normal facts of social life in the twelfth century.

20

explained according to the fashion of the Gothic world of its day. The reader is made constantly aware of the conflict between Christian doctrine and Christian duty and practice, and the stated assumptions and events of the poem. He would be a rash man who presumed to judge Gottfried's own opinions.

We are thus presented with a range of opinion and interest wider than historians have commonly allowed. We cannot hope to know how this range was reflected in mankind at large. Yet we can assert with some confidence that there were plenty of folk to whom 'religious' concerns as ordinarily defined meant little, but that it was a world in which a range of theological interest spread from the schools to the manor house, in which theological interest was more widespread, and culture more theologically conditioned by far, than in our own. After all, it is the literature least likely to reveal theological concerns which we have inspected.

PETER ABELARD'S AUTOBIOGRAPHY

We have modified our original statement about the age of faith almost out of recognition; yet it remains clear that we cannot travel far towards the heart of our renaissance without inspecting its schools, its theology, the hidden rivers from which scholasticism flowed. To these the indispensable guide is Abelard, and the best introduction to Abelard is his own autobiography, the *History of my Calamities*, and the letters of his wife, the Abbess Heloise. 'The medieval background could in my opinion for a time be best forgotten', wrote Hugh Sacker in his *Introduction to Wolfram's 'Parzival'*, 'and attention concentrated on the individual work.'[4] He was writing of the criticism of medieval German literature; but the same can be said of Latin literature as well. This may seem a paradoxical statement; and I certainly do not underestimate what we have learned of the rich background and world of assumptions of twelfth century literature of every kind from the intensive study of recent decades. But too exclusive a study of background, of *Geistesgeschichte*, of forms and models and traditions, can easily lead us to patronize, to attribute too much to 'sources', to lose track of real originality. It is the paradoxical consequence of Sacker's method that he makes the *Parzival* a much more revealing document of its world by treating it as an individual work not as a literary type: revealing of the range of thought and interest, of the originality, and depth of reflection, possible to a humble knight in that age. These qualities in turn reflect a basic fact about the twelfth century, that it saw the growth of a world far more varied and sophisticated than its predecessor.

Only thus too can we appreciate the creative urge of our renaissance. It is indeed a constant difficulty that a historian must study sources, influences and tradition, that his task makes too ready a surrender to the notion of originality or genius something akin to obscurantism: it can preclude all further enquiry. But he is not the slave of his materials or his techniques. There is no greater heresy than that good literature or good

art is the product of its sources or moulded entirely by tradition. Traditional literature exists, indeed: some or many of the epics of the early twelfth century, the *Chansons de Geste*, were oral poems recited and adapted by minstrels, based on a long tradition; it would be as absurd to look for originality in them as in the run of the mill theological commentaries of the next century. Yet even here a cool look at the work in its own right can help profoundly to elucidate its purpose: even where a medieval tradition dictated the form a modern tradition of criticism may serve to obscure the substance. We should read the literature of the twelfth century as its best minds read the works of the past: as fresh, new and living, as if they had not been read before. For it is this which makes the literature of the twelfth century worth our study and its culture our respect: like the humanists of the fifteenth century men took old books off the shelves of libraries, blew the dust off them and read them as if they were contemporary, just published. Thus they read Lucan and Virgil, Cicero and Macrobius, Aristotle and

6 Opposite, Boethius sitting with his tablets in the initial of the first book of *Consolations of Philosophy*, twelfth century

7 Left, Aristotle, from the west front of Chartres cathedral, mid-twelfth century

23

Boethius, St Augustine and St Paul, the *Remedy of Love* and the *Rule of St Benedict* – even the Bible itself. Needless to say, they revealed the tastes of their own world in doing so, as we all do; but they read none the less with new eyes. The meaning of this is revealed with special clarity in Abelard's book.

The basic facts seem to be as follows. Abelard in his later years felt called on to comfort a friend in trouble; and the urge called out a deeper emotion in that prince of egoists – the urge to self-expression, to self-analysis, to revealing his superiority even in sorrow. Your troubles are nothing to mine, he says in effect – so bluntly, not to say coolly, that it has been questioned whether the occasion of the book was not a polite fiction. He takes his friend on a tour of the schools in which he had studied so ardently: to Paris, to Laon, and back to Paris. Everywhere, he says, I rapidly surpassed my masters in disputation and so won their envy: the more my fame grew, the more men hated me. To make matters worse, after a while I fell head-over-heels in love with a charming girl of great intelligence, whose uncle and guardian eventually had me castrated in his rage. Then she and I both took to the monastic life; but I soon found the abbey of Saint-Denis dishearteningly lax and irregular. I tried to live the life of a hermit of the desert, but students found me out and I became, perforce, a teacher once again. And so the story goes on, of his quarrels with his communities, his successes, his arrogance and the enemies it won him; of persecution by fellow teachers – and the first condemnation of his books at Soissons in 1121 – and by his fellow monks. The story is told with extraordinary plainness and lucidity; with a strange mingling of detachment and involved self-pity; not without irony, self-criticism and repentance; yet always harping on the wrong-headedness of his opponents. Understandably, it was kept to a restricted circle in his lifetime; but it fell into the hands of Heloise, now an abbess, once his wife and lover, and drew from her the first of a series of letters even more extraordinary than the book itself.

Abelard tells us that his father, Berengar, was a Breton knight who had loved letters before he took to arms, and ended his life in a monastic community. His father first sent him to school; and Abelard quickly fell in love with learning, so that he left home and his inheritance and wandered from place to place in search of argument, 'disputando', 'imitating the wandering scholars'* of Aristotle's school 'wherever I heard that the study of the art [of disputation] flourished'. A generation later another of the great egotists of the twelfth century, Gerald of Wales, the immortal archdeacon, described in his autobiography how the Norman marcher lord, his father, observed his sons building sandcastles – but Gerald traced cathedrals and great churches in the sand, and so his father called him 'my bishop' and set him to letters.

Nothing is more striking in the history of the twelfth century schools than the rapid increase in the numbers of students who flocked to them. We are very ill informed where they came from. Gerald's father was a baron, his mother a Welsh princess. In the Anglo–Norman world, with some striking exceptions, the high nobility seem to have held a prejudice against a clerical career for their sons – though sometimes very generous in supporting other folk's sons in the schools – and not many were to be found even of Gerald's standing. In some parts of Europe the reverse was true, so that the local nobility, for example, round Cologne, had almost a monopoly of the stalls in the cathedral chapter. Abelard's family was a more characteristic source: his father was, as we should say of a later age, a member of the lesser gentry, well enough off to lend some support to sons who studied, capable in the long run of helping them to patronage if they needed it. Several of the characters in this book are known to have come from the gentry; others from the growing and flourishing burgess communities.

* The *Peripatetics*, who wandered as they talked, but were not wandering in Abelard's sense, of course.

8, 9, 10 The Professions, from the Reuner Muster-buch, *c.* 1208–18. From left to right: artisans (weavers at work); prosperous peasants (a farmer, perhaps a village reeve, supervises his ploughmen); craftsmen (scribe and painter)

Of the large majority we know nothing; but we shall not be far astray in reckoning that most came from the middling strata in society, gentry, merchants, well-to-do artisans, free and prosperous peasantry. Many were poorer than this, if we may believe their songs and their letters: but poverty has been as constant a theme among students as has decadence among their seniors since the first syllable of recorded time. All over western Christendom population was rising; and in a somewhat more settled society many younger sons had their living to seek. The opportunities were widening. For those who sought a life of war in the tradition of the feudal classes, the chance of employment as a mercenary was increasing; for those who liked war tinged with religious fanaticism, the crusades had a special appeal; for those who enjoyed physical adventures but felt no call to slaughter, there was the life of a merchant or a pilgrim; those who liked peace and calm were drawn to the older monastic communities; those who liked peace combined with something *avant-garde* in the religious life – who felt the common revulsion against growing wealth and higher material standards in the world at large – heard the call of the new orders, led by the Cistercians; those who looked for adventures of mind as well as body could find them in the search for the best techniques, the most lively schools.

11 The orders of society. A squire attends a knight who presents property to the Dean of Sainte-Croix-d'Orléans, for his dependent church at Mervilliers, whose priest celebrates Mass while a scribe writes the charter

Abelard was not a younger son; nor can he be fitted into any social mould; and he himself was to become the greatest attraction of all among the teachers of the age. But it is clear from his own account that there were many like him already at the outset of his career; many on the move from place to place, from teacher to teacher, school to school. Formal organization existed in embryo here and there, but the rise of universities, recognized centres of learning with special rights to issue degrees – schools to which students would flock irrespective of the reputation of individual teachers – was an event of the late twelfth and thirteenth centuries. The early twelfth century was the age *par excellence* of the wandering scholar, and masters who could teach the elements of learning were widely scattered. At an early age Abelard acquired a love of the special mental tool of the age and the man: dialectic, as we should say, logic. But he also acquired a considerable Latin culture and a Latin style of exceptional clarity and force. He did not trouble to tell us where he learned grammar and rhetoric, as the contemporary jargon described these fields of learning;★ and a similar obscurity surrounds the formation of the greatest master of rhetoric of the century, Abelard's younger contemporary and antagonist, St Bernard of Clairvaux.

Even then, learning was in some measure dependent on libraries, traditions and organization. The Church had the basic framework of an organization in cathedral schools, governed, under the bishop, by cathedral chancellors or 'masters of the schools' of a diocese. The main repositories of ancient learning were the libraries of cathedrals and monasteries – especially, in the centuries following the Carolingian renaissance (the ninth to the eleventh), in cathedrals. In the late tenth century the chief centre had been Rheims, where the

★ The basis of learning was the seven liberal arts: the 'trivium', grammar, rhetoric and logic (dialectic), which were the essential foundations; and the 'quadrivium', geometry, arithmetic, astronomy and music, which were studied less seriously. Beyond these lay the higher studies, especially theology and canon law, less commonly medicine.

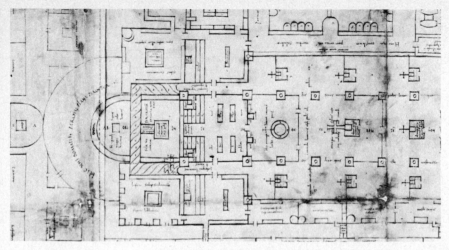

12 In the ninth-century plan of an imaginary monastery, in the library of St Gallen, the library is placed above the scriptorium to the north of the high altar – i.e. towards the bottom left of the detail shown here

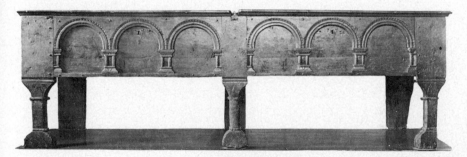

13, 14 A wooden book cupboard, now in the Musée de Valère, Sion (Switzerland), and, right, a book cupboard let into the cloister wall in the Augustinian abbey of Lilleshall (Shropshire) – both twelfth century

most learned man of the age, the encyclopedic Gerbert, had taught first as master, later as archbishop. Rheims was revived, along with several centres further north, such as Liège, in the course of the eleventh century. A more substantial tradition of learning, and a fine library, were set up at Chartres early in the eleventh century by Bishop Fulbert, a genial master, many of whose letters survive, written in the restricted, difficult but correct Latin of their period, revealing a desperate struggle to maintain civilized standards of conduct and pastoral care in a barbarous age, and the warmth of friendship between the master and his pupils. In many parts of Europe by the end of the century – in Germany and Italy as well as in France – we find evidence of a new, freer, richer Latin literature and of larger groups of students gathering at the feet of masters whose fame, by some means or other, could spread rapidly from land to land.

LOGIC

The learning of the early Middle Ages had been encyclopedic: its aim was to accumulate the stores of ancient learning, the aim of education to gather the materials to absorb, understand and enjoy the benefits of this learning. The horizons are bound to appear to us desperately narrow: yet the scholars of the twelfth century had inherited from the late Roman world – that is, from the early Christian world – a notion of a liberal education in its own way far wider than anything immediately conceivable in the fanatically specialized milieu of British education in the 1960s. What lent a special excitement to the chase was the discovery not only that ancient authorities disagreed, but that there was a toolchest of finely tempered tools for discerning where the discrepancies lay and for reconciling them. The new dialectic had reared its head in the strange type of logic developed by the most brilliant of the products of Chartres in the eleventh century, Berengar of Tours, who found the roots of logic in grammar and the meanings and

15 Fulbert, Bishop of Chartres (d. 1028), in his cathedral; from the memorial volume (now lost) prepared shortly after his death

16 Lanfranc, Prior of Bec, Abbot of Caen, and Archbishop of Canterbury (1070–89), from a twelfth century manuscript of his reply to Berengar of Tours

17 Hugh of Saint-Victor (*fl. c.* 1125–41), head of the school of Saint-Victor at Paris, mother house of the Victorine congregation of Augustinian canons; from a thirteenth century manuscript of one of his works, *De arca Morali*

declensions of words. This led him into eucharistic speculations which were in due course countered by Lanfranc, the Italian teacher who settled in the mid-eleventh century in the abbey of Bec in Normandy, and made a remote and poor house the centre of a flourishing school as Abelard was later to do at Saint-Gildas. Lanfranc was a profound believer in authority, as he showed at the end of his life in another sphere where he made a deep mark, as William the Conqueror's archbishop of Canterbury (1070–89). He developed his logical tools with authorities always in mind. His pupil at Bec, and successor at Canterbury, Anselm of Aosta, was one of the world's most brilliant philosophers. He believed himself entirely wrapped up in authorities, but in practice his mind was of such a temper that it pursued its own original way in blissful ignorance of its own originality. Thus he developed out of the tradition of Platonic 'ideas' a new, ethereal argument for God's existence. The 'idea' of God is unique; and if we grant this, then we can show that the Fool who says there is no God contradicts himself.[5] Late in life he took advantage of the release from his duties as archbishop produced by a clash with King William II, quietly and happily, in his greatest book, to blow away the cobwebs which surrounded the doctrine of the Atonement.

In the mid and late twelfth century great compilations of authorities were made, and the dialectical tools considerably refined. In the process a vast number of traditional solutions were established, and the channels of intellectual advance became narrower. Thus the intellectual tradition in which St Thomas Aquinas was reared in the mid-thirteenth century was at once more sophisticated, far more sophisticated, than Abelard's, but also less broad and less open. Abelard's natural instinct, like Anselm's, was to follow the bent of his own mind, and he worked, like Anselm, in the brief interval during which the tools were being refined but the elaborate tradition of scholastic craftsmanship had not been formed.

Abelard reckoned the key movement in his own develop-ment to be his arrival at Paris, already a distinguished school, and one which he himself was to make the most famous in Europe. There he studied under a leading figure of the Paris establishment, William of Champeaux, first canon of Notre Dame and archdeacon of Paris, later canon regular in the religious house in Paris most frequented by scholars, Saint-Victor. William propounded his own solution to the burning philosophical issue of the day – the issue of 'universals'. The universal was the lineal successor to the Platonic 'idea', and in an intellectual world dominated by Plato – though, oddly enough, Plato studied almost entirely at second hand through his Roman pupils – the reality of 'ideas' and of groups or classes of phenomena, or 'universals', was accepted orthodoxy. Voices were raised in criticism of this, and William attempted to lead his pupils to faith in his own solution. Abelard, helpful as ever, found a hole in his master's case, and expected a grateful response to this revelation. He tried to teach his master, and so made the first of many powerful enemies.

Abelard was the most brilliant pupil of the Platonic teachers of the eleventh and early twelfth centuries; and it is therefore not altogether surprising that his solution of this basic philosophical problem was akin to that of Plato's most eminent pupil, Aristotle. In course of time this became apparent, for the eager search for ancient learning led in the course of the twelfth and thirteenth centuries to the recovery and intensive study of a great part of Aristotle's works. Adventurous scholars like Adelard of Bath travelled in the fringes of the Latin, Greek and Moslem worlds and found many traces of Greek and Latin literature long forgotten – in particular the scientific works of Euclid and Aristotle. It was partly the scientific and philosophical bent of these explorers – but partly, it must be said, a tangle of causes which has not been unravelled – which made Aristotle the centre of this new-found literature, not Homer or Aeschylus or Euripides. These ancient works were discovered both in the Arab world, which had long absorbed far more of Greek culture than the west, and in the Greek world itself, in Byzantium and above all in Sicily, where

35

perfini   callarū

alba   Scenārchadū   castrū mari

post sarrazins

⌐notarii Greci⌐ ⌐Not saraceni⌐   ⌐not latini⌐   Bigam' nocte scribes
tancredS.

18, 19 The capital and court of Sicily, from a manuscript of 1195–6. Left, Palermo, its gardens, palatine chapel, port and castle, and the various peoples who lived in different quarters of the city. Above, the royal court: notaries writing in Greek, Arabic and Latin

Greek and Arab, Italian and Norman mingled in the new kingdom of Roger the Great. The impulse to translate was stirred also by the meeting of Christian and Moslem in Spain, where they had long coexisted, and where relations were only occasionally fouled by crusading rancour and fanaticism.

Most of this effort lay in the future when Abelard's mind was formed, and of far greater consequence to his outlook was the patient compilation of legal authorities characteristic of the last great master in Fulbert's school at Chartres[6] of the eleventh century, Ivo, bishop of Chartres (d. 1116). He and his disciples, faced with practical problems of pastoral care and administration, put together a large compilation of the authorities for canon law, the law of the Church, and then compressed it into a tidy and practical manual, the *Panormia*, which remained the most popular textbook of canon law for a generation or so. To both these works Ivo attached a preface, in

37

which he pointed out that authorities could appear to conflict, and laid down certain principles by which their conflicts might be resolved. Their actual resolution he left to younger men and a more mature scholarship. This technique inspired Abelard to his famous teaching manual, the *Sic et non*, 'Yes and no'. A preface outlines the principles; the book consists of a selection of conflicting texts. It was left to his pupils to resolve them, not because Abelard lacked confidence in his own ability, but because his aim was to teach; and this famous book, planned with dazzling simplicity to make his pupils think for themselves, enables us to gain some insight into the outrageous brilliance of his teaching, which made students flock to him from every part of western Christendom.

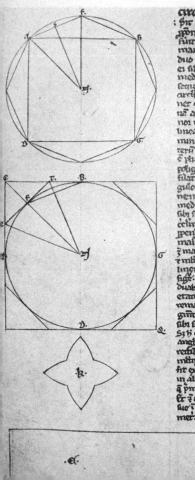

MEDIEVAL SCIENCE

These pictures illustrate the lively interest in science – still primitive and traditional, but concerned to revive ancient learning and, in a measure, based on observation

20 Euclidean geometry; from a thirteenth century manuscript

21 Surgery; treatment of the eye and nose from a twelfth century Herbal of Dioscorides

22 A peacock; from a twelfth century Bestiary

23 Blackberries; from an early twelfth century Herbal

The *Sic et non* was a text-book in the application of dialectic to theology. Abelard's first steps in this science were taken with Master Anselm of Laon, who had the highest reputation in the field, Abelard tells us, on account of his antiquity; and 'a wonderful flow of words he had, but their sense was despicable and empty of all rational argument. When he lit a fire, he filled his house with smoke; no illumination came.' Thus characteristically Abelard introduces us to the next of his persecutors. But Anselm and his circle are not so readily dismissed. They were the fundamental accumulators of ancient learning in this field, and on their work, as much as on Abelard's dialectic, the future of scholasticism was to rest. The word theology for something approaching a systematic study was indeed coined by Abelard. But the field of learning as then commonly defined was reckoned to consist fundamentally in the study of the 'Sacred Page', that is, of the Bible; and the achievement of the school of Laon lay in collecting innumerable glosses from earlier commentaries on the Bible, selecting and arranging and putting into circulation something approaching a standard corpus of exegetical learning, particularly the learning of the Fathers. This came to be known as the Ordinary Gloss, the *Glossa Ordinaria*; it was copied a hundredfold and many times more, and became the basic stock-in-trade of every theological library. One can see why Anselm of Laon did not inspire Abelard: his work in its content was wholly unoriginal; he and his colleagues and pupils were encyclopedists, not original thinkers. But their work lasted and gave foundation for the far more elaborate commentaries of the next generation and the far more sophisticated commentaries of the end of the century. The climax of twelfth century Biblical commentaries was the work of Stephen Langton, professor at Paris, later cardinal and archbishop of Canterbury (1207–28); author also of the Golden Sequence, and perhaps in a measure too of *Magna Carta*.

24 The *Glossa Ordinaria*. A portion of Leviticus from a twelfth century glossed Bible: the main gloss in the left-hand margin includes quotations from 'Adamantius' (Origen) and Ambrosius (St Ambrose)

The other fundamental text-book of theology of the century was the *Liber Sententiarum*, the *Sentences* of Peter the Lombard, completed at Paris about 1150. In the *Sic et non* Abelard had laid out the tools and the problems, advancing along lines indicated by Ivo of Chartres. In Abelard's later years his techniques and those of others of his day who enjoyed contemporary dialectic were carried back into the field of canon law by Master Gratian of Bologna, whose *Decretum*, also called the *Concord of Discordant Canons*, was first issued about 1140, and placed together, on a scale never attempted before, a collection of authorities even larger than Ivo's, and a flowing argument which might have won admiration even from Abelard. About the same time the young Italian scholar Peter the Lombard moved to Paris and there combined the learning and the techniques of Bologna and Paris in the *Sentences*, which did for the problems of theology precisely what Gratian had done for canon law. Gratian's was the more original mind: for all the foundations laid by Ivo and others, it was he who started serious speculation on a number of legal issues, and created the science in a manner comparable to

41

Adam Smith's creation of economics. His intention was to make warring authorities concur. The Lombard had not only warring authorities but warring theologians on his hands. 'Under the placid exterior of a text-book', writes R. W. Southern, 'the *Sentences* are alive with the intense and questioning intellectual life of the time. In many ways it was not a very attractive intellectual life: little men with little dialectical gimlets were offering to open all the safes in the theological world.'[7] The Lombard combined a calm assurance which appealed to conservatives like St Bernard – who, indeed, introduced him to Paris as a counter to the evil influences (as he conceived them) of Abelard and his brood. He also had a shrewd eye for the real problems, as the twelfth century saw them, and a notable skill in clear arrangement and exposition, which made his stately array of authorities a magnificent toolchest, and ensured that the theologians of the next generation did not have to be content with gimlets. And not only of the next generation; for the *Decretum* and the *Sentences* have had a unique career as best sellers. The Lombard's book remained the foundation of theological study down to the seventeenth century, Gratian's of canon law down to the twentieth. In the educational techniques of the schools, these two books made a greater ripple than the Reformation; and it is astonishing to reflect how long was the road that led from Ivo, via Abelard and Gratian, to the Lombard, and how rapidly traversed.

A closer look at Gratian's world in Bologna will help to make this more intelligible (see pp. 75 ff.). Meanwhile we can see that a group of minds of exceptional freshness, versatility and insight were needed to prepare the change. Of these, both as teacher and as theologian, the greatest was Abelard; but it would be absurd to attribute everything to Abelard alone. It may indeed seem absurd to a twentieth century reader to make so much of the difference between the theology of 1100 and of 1150. Yet a glance at the difference in views of the Atonement and of morality can bring it home to us. Of the

25 Christ the Ruler. This twelfth century book-cover of Limoges enamel is a characteristic example of the tradition of Christ enthroned, between alpha and omega, with the symbols of the Evangelists, as described in the Apocalypse

person of Jesus two views were held in the central Middle Ages. He was the ruler and judge, who triumphed and ruled from the Cross, and judged all men at the last day. Innumerable representations of the Crucifixion and the Last Judgment bear witness to this; and they link with the traditional, monastic, ascetic view of human destiny. The world was God's world, hence good; but corrupted by the Fall and by sin to the point that it made little difference whether one believed, with the orthodox, that the Devil had merely corrupted the world, or with the Cathar heretics – very numerous in western Christendom from the mid-twelfth century on – that the material world was the Devil's creation. In the art of the early

43

26 Satan as a fallen angel; from the Temptation of Jesus in the Munich Gospels of Otto III, *c*. 1000

27 The Demonic Satan from the mouth of Hell in the Psalter of Henry of Blois, *c*. 1150–60

28 Gilbert's Satan, tempting Christ in Autun cathedral, early twelfth century

29 The comic devil from the Bohemian Codex Gigas, early thirteenth century

eleventh century Satan has the dignity of a fallen angel; in the late eleventh and twelfth he became a fearful and sometimes a comic monster.

To most men in the eleventh century, however strongly charity and faith might burn, hope was small. 'Few will be saved', thought St Anselm, 'and most of these will be monks.'[8] The Devil had established dominion over men; and it was even held that this demonic empire involved rights to which God felt bound. Earlier views of the Atonement turned on how God could break the Devil's rights. Through this net Anselm himself cut a clear passage: the Devil could have no rights. But the Devil's *de facto* rule was a fact of experience to Anselm, and in his *Cur Deus Homo* he deliberately held back from any view which made the Incarnation an act of Divine love bringing hope to the many. This strange combination of logical insight and theological conservatism in his eminent

45

These plates show the growing
interest in the human sufferings
of Jesus, and his patronage of
human activities and aspirations

30 The deposition from the
Cross; from an ivory, probably
Spanish, of the eleventh or
twelfth century

31 Jesus, both crowned and
suffering; from a wooden cross
at Vich (Barcelona), twelfth or
thirteenth century

32 Jesus as a pilgrim; from a
French manuscript of the
twelfth century

33 Jesus as a knight; from the
silver reliquary of Saint-Hadelin,
in the church of Saint-Martin,
Vise (Belgium), eleventh
century

predecessor helped to inspire Abelard to a considerable feat of gymnastics. His account of the Atonement held nothing of traditional doctrine: it was not an act by the Divine Judge, but the launching of the human Jesus, to be a companion and example to men. Abelard's doctrine appeared to his successors as one-sided as he and they agreed to think the old, legalistic view. But it lifted a curtain in theological debate and let in some light from the wider field of religious sentiment. A new theme appeared in religious art in the eleventh century: the suffering Jesus, with a human mother whose cult was beginning to flourish in a new way; the God made man who lived in a particular part of the globe, which could be visited by

47

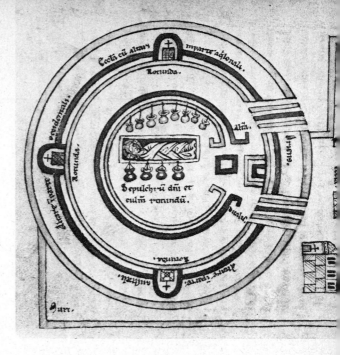

34 This map from a thirteenth century English psalter shows Jerusalem in the centre of the world as God sees it

35 The Church of the Holy Sepulchre, Jerusalem, from an early thirteenth century copy of a guide book; it was the model for round churches in western Europe

adventurous pilgrims and recovered for Christendom by dedicated Crusaders.

In moral teaching Abelard laid a similarly new emphasis, also one-sided, but fundamental to any theological advance. The human will and its intention were vital to his view of the moral spring of action; to the objective act, seen in the eyes of God, he paid little attention. Once again, man's viewpoint and his relation to a God who loves rather than judges are given a quite new emphasis. No doubt Abelard jumped too readily to new conclusions, and often sacrificed depth for brilliance of insight; no doubt, too, he was an arrogant, self-willed man who paid altogether exaggerated homage to his own emotions. But it will not do to see him as a carnal man of superficial brilliance; as a man who had dialectical insight without theological understanding; or as a man wholly lacking in spiritual depth. As with many people of high ability and strong character, several men lived under his skin. One at least of these had exceptional insight into genuine theological

49

problems. He could engage in speculations of a quite untheological character, as when he likened the persons of the Trinity to qualities in Greek philosophy. He could show a startling inadvertence in expressing his conclusions. But he firmly grasped the idea that the God of love had wished to save all men, even though the Fall frustrated Him; that God made man was deeply concerned with human emotions and human values; and he even caught the hem of the notion – so difficult for professional theologians ever to comprehend – that the Christian cannot be satisfied with a God whose moral standard is lower than his own.

HELOISE

No doubt there is a paradox in elevating a man whose immortal fame rests on his skill in the art of seduction into a great moral theologian. Even in the late twentieth century one can say that his life and his doctrine were inadequate. Yet his insights were genuine and profound, and he owed this, we need not doubt, in large measure to his relations with Heloise. As a thinker, Heloise is indistinguishable from Abelard: she sank her own mind so deeply in his that she wrote in his style and her letters have been thought to be of his composition. As a personality she is more interesting than he, and far more attractive; yet terrifying too, for her passionate self-analysis lays a whole range of human experience bare in a way which can hardly be paralleled in the Middle Ages. In an age in which an interest in human emotion and self-expression was growing in a limited, but not confined, circle of sophisticated minds, Abelard and Heloise developed this capacity to an extreme point. It is no chance that their letters hardly circulated at all in the twelfth century but were of intense interest to Petrarch in the fourteenth century and to Pope in the eighteenth. For they lived in imagination in the world of classical Stoic philosophy, intensely felt and brilliantly expressed. In this sense, their own account of their relations is a remarkable expression of medieval humanism in two senses of the word: love of the ancient world and concern for human emotions and their expression. But their relations also brought out one of the central problems of the twelfth century: the links and contradictions between love human and divine.

In the *Historia Calamitatum* Abelard describes his affair and his marriage at some length, though not so as to dominate his other persecutions. He treats his wife with respect, and gives a notably full account of her attempt to dissuade him from marriage – she would rather be his mistress than his wife, since marriage would mean disgrace and an end to his career. But the incident is closed: she is now a respectable abbess, he a much persecuted abbot. Fulbert's ruffians had made carnal union impossible, and they had dissolved their marriage in the only way open to them, by both entering religious communities. Their union is a thing of the past. Heloise was considerably the younger of the two, and her whole being was wrapped up in her relations with Abelard: she reveals, with horrifying clarity, the idolatrous nature of her attitude to him. She enjoyed their intercourse, and still pines for what she has lost; obedience to him is the mainspring of her actions, and that is the only reason why she is an abbess. She is still his wife first and foremost. It is easy to take her too literally. All this is said in the context of a passionate self-accusation: she is reckoned a model abbess; in point of fact she is a miserable sinner; the curse of Eve is upon her. But Abelard confirms her gift for the vivid imaginative vision of her own role. When she stood before the bishop to take the veil, he tells us, her friends tried to dissuade her; but she obeyed her husband's will, making it clear that she did so in the spirit of the Stoic Cornelia in Lucan's poem: 'O most renowned of husbands. . . . Accept from me the penalty which I pay of my free choice'[9] – in a spirit, that is, of tragic despair, not of Christian faith and hope. In their correspondence Abelard tried to draw her love for him into the world of God's love, but she at first resisted, pointing out ruthlessly the ambiguities and difficulties in seeing analogies between them. Thus, in a way, we are prepared both for the analogy of human and divine love which forms the central message of hope in the writings of St Bernard and did so much to make the outlook of the faithful more optimistic, to revive the doctrine and the sentiment of hope; and also for the parody and inversion of this analogy which forms the theme of many of the courtly romances.

It is a mistake to spoil these letters by summary: they must be read, and read whole. They do not always make easy reading, for Heloise was as learned as incisive; but she was in all things exceptional, as an educated lady and a daughter of the close, as a humanist, as a unique exponent of the doctrine and the practice of marriage. These are the themes of the chapters which follow. As a tormented wife and abbess we must now take leave of her; though the world would have been the poorer if she had not been all these things.

The *Historia Calamitatum* had a sequel. In the 1130s Abelard's fame was as great as ever, his pen even more active than before. But his influence, the fertility of his mind and its originality, stirred the fears as well as the envy of more conservative men. In 1140 they enlisted the most powerful controversialist of the age, Bernard of Clairvaux, a younger man than Abelard, and no match for him in open debate; but by a mixture of prayer and intrigue which modern observers find impossible to forgive, the saintly abbot brought Abelard to his second condemnation. From the Council of Sens he set forth to appeal to Rome; but he found consolation sooner than expected. Two years later the abbot of Cluny wrote to the Abbess Heloise to tell her of the last act of her husband's life. Peter the Venerable was the most courtly of twelfth century letter writers; but there is an intense and moving sympathy about this letter which shows that Abelard in his last months, however broken in spirit, was still capable of drawing from a dedicated monk an insight into the nature of Christian marriage of a profundity wholly exceptional in that ascetic world.[10]

PATRONS AND PATRONAGE

In Abelard and Heloise we have met theology and humanism in the French capital of the twelfth century Renaissance. But what do we mean by humanism? What do we mean by French? These questions can best be answered by tracing the career of John of Salisbury, who was a humanist in more senses than one, an Englishman, and yet also at home, very much at home, in Paris, Rheims and Rome.

Old Sarum, the birthplace of John of Salisbury, is today a unique reminder of the spirit of Norman England. The bishopric of Dorset and Wiltshire had been moved in the 1070s by Bishop Herman, in accordance with the policy of the Norman bishops, to a fortified town; and he had chosen this magnificent prehistoric hill-fort, still protected by ancient ramparts. It was just large enough to include a substantial castle, a fine cathedral and the tumble of little houses which eleventh century man dignified by the name of a town. It was dominated by the castle, a royal castle, though often administered by the bishop, and by the cathedral; and the alliance of chapter and garrison suited the circumstances of early Norman times – of Norman conquerors ill at ease in the English countryside, or of Henry I's Bishop Roger, the great administrator, who combined Church and State in his own person; but was hardly congenial to the more peaceful atmosphere or higher living standards of the late twelfth century. In the early thirteenth century the brothers Herbert and Richard Poore, distant relatives perhaps of Bishop Roger but men of different temper, presided over the transfer of the see and town to its new site by the Avon, where cathedral and close could

53

enjoy more ample grounds, and where a plentiful supply of water lay to hand. And so Old Sarum is deserted, and we can inspect the small world in which John of Salisbury was brought up, undistracted by the housing schemes of later generations.

It was a very small world, and yet hardly parochial. We do not know what calling his father followed – a tradesman, perhaps, or a cleric – but it is clear that, though his origin was not unduly humble, his livelihood always depended till the very end of his life on patronage. The dominant figure at Old Sarum in John's childhood was the formidable Bishop Roger, who lived there – when the business of king and kingdom allowed him – with his wife or concubine, Matilda of Ramsbury, surrounded by the leading clergy of the cathedral, all of them linked to Roger and Matilda by ties of family or patronage. Their son, Roger the 'Poor', for a time royal chancellor, was brought up there and Bishop Roger's nephews Nigel, later royal treasurer and bishop of Ely, and Alexander the 'Magnificent', later bishop of Lincoln, were canons and archdeacons. At the end of Roger's life Azo of Ramsbury, clearly a connection of Matilda's, was dean of the Cathedral; his brother Roger[11] held one of the archdeaconries. A married bishop was an anachronism and an abuse in the early twelfth century; the papal reformers of the previous two generations had campaigned for the celibacy of the clergy, not wholly without success. But Matilda's role was not altogether disreputable in that age, even though the little we know of her suggests that she was more of a Brunhild than an Isolde; nor was Roger's dynasty the only large clerical connection to be found in western Christendom. Roger and his nephews were worldly churchmen; yet the idealism of the papal reform had its representatives in their chapter too. An earlier dean, Serlo, left Salisbury to become a canon regular in the 1120s and rose to be abbot of Henry I's great foundation for Augustinian Canons at Cirencester in 1131. Meanwhile the precentor, Godwin, who lived and died at Sarum, was composing meditations of a notable piety for his own immediate circle. It was in just such a world, of old established domesticity and new idealism, that Heloise had been brought up in the house of her uncle, Canon Fulbert, in the close at Paris; and this world, in which love for a student and marriage for a clerk were fashionable and customary – yet violently denounced by the Church's leaders – helps to explain the tangle of Abelard's life.

The impression from his childhood which stayed with John of Salisbury was not the domesticity of Bishop Roger's affinity, but its place in the spider's web of patronage. At the centre of the web was the king, Henry I, who largely founded his government on a complex system which brought royal patronage at first or second hand to a fair proportion of

36 Old Sarum. The site of John of Salisbury's birthplace, with the Norman castle and cathedral set in ancient ramparts

37 The Great Seal of Henry II, of which Thomas Becket as chancellor was custodian (British Museum cast). This side shows the king on horseback; on the obverse he is enthroned with sword and orb

the folk who mattered, clerics as well as layfolk. As Henry's closest associate among the clergy – save perhaps, in later years, for the king's nephew, Henry of Blois, bishop of Winchester – Bishop Roger naturally commanded an ample field of patronage for himself and his associates. When Henry died, the web decayed, and was almost blown away; Roger himself fell into disgrace and died in 1139. By then John was in his mid-teens, and a mature student in the cosmopolitan world of northern France. But he never forgot that his life depended on patronage, and after twelve years of broad and deep study he returned to England, with a testimonial from St Bernard of Clairvaux, to join the household of Theobald, archbishop of Canterbury. From 1148 to 1176, though a frequent visitor in the 1150s to the papal court, and an exile for most of the 1160s, his fate was linked with successive archbishops, Theobald, Thomas Becket and Richard of Dover, and he lived a life in which learning and administration were inextricably mingled. Finally, in 1176, King Louis VII of France paid tribute to his respect for John's learning and the memory of the martyred Thomas Becket, by summoning him to be bishop of Chartres. There John presided over an old library and an old cathedral, which was already, however, a storehouse of twelfth century art, until his death in 1180.

John and Becket both made their way in practical affairs in the brilliant circle gathered round Archbishop Theobald. Both accepted without question the world of patronage on which their livelihood depended. But Thomas, the son of a citizen of London of knightly family, knew more of the world, and was more aware of the tensions that could arise between the new type of higher clergy – celibate, highly educated, brought up to accept the rule of the pope as well of the king – and the upper laymen, still half literate (like Henry II or Abelard's father) or illiterate, as most of them were. In the first two or three years after Henry II's accession the sun seemed to shine on Thomas and John alike. Thomas combined the highest office under the archbishop as archdeacon of Canterbury, and the highest clerical office under the king, as royal chancellor. No doubt the panache and ostentation of Becket's style of life brought uneasy memories of Bishop Roger; yet John, with half his mind, fully accepted the world of patronage, and reckoned to climb in it himself with Thomas' and Theobald's aid. In 1155–56 his opportunity came. Henry II was dreaming imperial dreams in which all the claims of his family entered – from the south of France to Ireland. He needed an ambassador to Rome to seek the consent for an Irish adventure of the pope, who had a rival claim to over-lordship of islands not tightly bound into the structure of European kingship. The chancellor's friend, the archbishop's expert in papal affairs, was also a friend of the pope, the English Adrian IV (1154–59). John was sent, and the prospect of

38 Signatures of Pope and Cardinals to a bull of Adrian IV. The cross at the top of the 'rota' (the circle) and possibly the 'E' of Ego . . . were written by the pope himself

reward, at Westminster and at Rome, must have seemed bright. Yet neither came to pass. It is likely indeed that Adrian meditated making John a cardinal; but he died before the scheme came to fruition. As for Henry, he concluded that John had sold the pass to Rome, and was highly incensed. What really happened is quite obscure; but perhaps the most likely explanation is that Henry wished merely to have the pope's consent for his enterprise, and that Adrian responded with a conditional gift, treating Ireland as a papal domain making nothing of Henry's precious claims. Though the archbishop harboured no resentment, and indeed made John his principal secretary at about this time, John himself felt all the bitterness of failure, and the lure of the royal court from which he was for a time excluded.

39 John of Salisbury's *Entheticus*; the earliest manuscript, perhaps written in John's lifetime. It belonged to the eminent bibliophile Simon, abbot of St Albans (1167–83)

JOHN'S BOOKS

His reaction to this disaster was to write a large book expounding the principles on which royal government and politics should be conducted. The *Policraticus, or courtiers' trifles and philosophers' footprints*, seems to have grown out of a larger scheme of encyclopedic learning. Of this two other fragments survive: a first draft of the *Policraticus* in the satirical poem, the *Entheticus*; and a study of quite another topic, the teaching of logic and its place in the larger scheme of learning, in the *Metalogicon*. On these works, and especially on the *Policraticus*, which is far the largest of them, John's fame as a scholar mainly depends. He also wrote a vivid fragment of a chronicle, *Memoirs of the papal Court*, a few short tracts, a life of St Anselm and a life of St Thomas Becket, and a large number of letters. These other works earn him the reputation of being a brilliant historian manqué, one of the most perfunctory of biographers and one of the most successful letter writers of a great period of biography and letters.

In a famous passage in the *Metalogicon* John described his education in the French schools. His account is more succinct and more urbane than Abelard's – though John could wield the rapier when he wished; but the abiding impression is that John, entering the schools of Paris* a generation later than Abelard, at the stage, indeed, when Abelard's own career was drawing to a close, found them far more diverse and mature than they could have been a generation earlier. Between 1136 and 1148 John absorbed everything which the teachers and the libraries of the Île de France had to offer; and he spent much time in studying dialectic and theology. But the studies which impressed him most deeply were those in the tradition that led back through his own teacher William of Conches to William's master Bernard of Chartres. Bernard is one of those men, like a character in Dickens, who has become immortal for a single saying. The moderns are to the ancients, John reports him to have said, as a dwarf on the shoulders of a giant. If the dwarf holds his seat, he can indeed see further than the giant; and thus was expressed the confidence of the twelfth century schools that if they founded their work on the right *authorities* knowledge would advance. Here we come face to face with the special devotion of Bernard and his followers to ancient learning, which was one of the genuine links between the twelfth and the fifteenth centuries.

John likened the functioning of a kingdom to a human body, and attributed the analogy to a book by Plutarch dedicated

* Or, as is usually said, the schools of Paris and Chartres. In a paper given to the Ecclesiastical History Society Conference in Oxford in 1965 and shortly to be published, Professor R. W. Southern showed reason to doubt whether the scholars associated with the famous 'school of Chartres' in the twelfth century actually taught in that city; the literary and philosophical tradition associated with it may well have flourished in Paris in John's time.

to the Emperor Trajan. We now know that this book was a polite fiction, invented by John to lend a mysterious antiquity to speculations based partly on the teaching of an English theologian, Robert Pullen, whose lectures John had attended in Paris, and partly on the scientific and cosmological speculations of William of Conches. Plutarch, furthermore, was a pagan, and enables John to construct his analogy as a piece of natural philosophy, not dependent on Christian revelation. John's learning in the pagan classics was extraordinarily wide and deep.

If he enjoyed puzzling his readers by referring them to bogus antiquities, he also enjoyed puzzling them by reference to ancient works of extreme obscurity. He was the only scholar between the fall of Rome and Petrarch to show any knowledge of Petronius' *Dream of Trimalchio*: 'Enter Trimalchio's feast in Petronius', he said on one occasion, '– if you can'. This is an innocent example of John in boastful mood. But the final impression, characteristic of John's circle as well as of John himself, is that the pagan classics are appreciated because they feed a mind profoundly and decisively Christian. The *Policraticus* is full of good advice to secular rulers and to courtiers: it bores a modern reader by deploying endless instances of ancient political wisdom, and very rarely citing examples from its own world. Yet it was very actual to John's own situation. Of the body of the common weal the king may be head; but the priests are its soul – and kings are members of a Christian commonwealth of which the pope is the head, under Christ. John was a courtier by instinct. As he was preparing the *Policraticus* he came across Boethius' *Consolations of Philosophy*, written by a greater courtier than John as he awaited execution at the orders of Theodoric the Ostrogoth, while the last vestiges of Roman greatness struggled with barbarism for mastery in sixth century Italy. Here was a book which answered his condition perfectly: for did he not share Boethius' conjunction of philosophic calm and personal and political martyrdom?

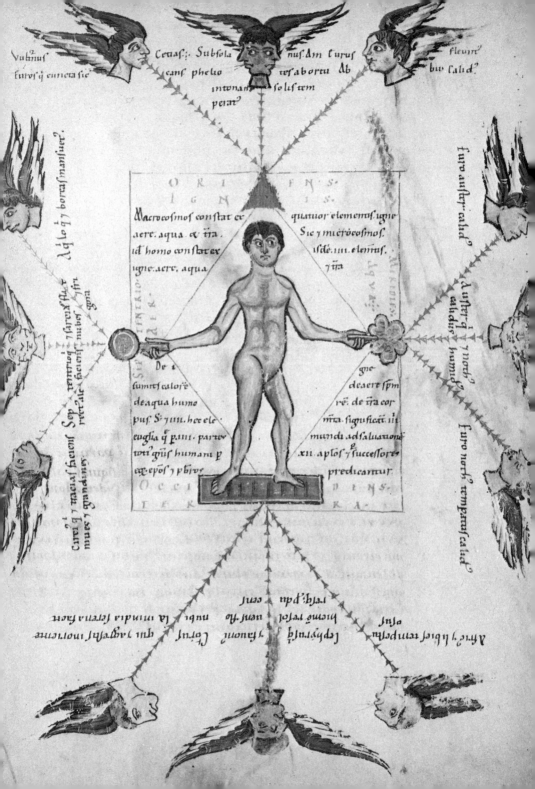

The analogy seems to us absurd; yet it was not wholly so. After Archbishop Theobald's death and Becket's accession, John joined the staff of the new archbishop, his old friend – the man to whom *Policraticus* and *Metalogicon* had been dedicated. Within a short space of time Thomas Becket, no longer the pliant civil servant, was at loggerheads with Henry II. 'You are my lord,' he told Henry in one of his letters, 'you are my king; you are my spiritual son'; and the final clause divided them. Henry expected obedience from a faithful subject; Becket insisted that there were realms where he must lead, where Henry was not his master, where he must obey pope, rather than king. From 1164 to 1170 Thomas was an exile in the Île de France, John at Rheims, an honoured guest of his closest friend, outside the circle of his family, Peter of Celle, abbot of Saint-Rémi. From this period stems the second and larger collection of John's letters; and their constant themes are his wish to return to the world of English patronage, his stubborn refusal to surrender in his support of archbishop and pope, his pursuit of friendship, and his Christian humanism.

In spite of his friendship with Becket and his memories of the 1150s, John at first found it hard to believe that there could be a schism in the small world of educated English clerks, whose centre had lain in Theobald's household – and who still looked to the royal court as the capital of the world of patronage on which their livelihood depended. He wrote freely to men who supported the king against Becket asking for their help; he was ready to do anything consistent with conscience and his debt to the archbishop that would enable him to return. There is a distinctly unheroic strain in these early letters. They have, that is, the mark of a genuine human situation; and thus they share with the letters of Heloise an exceptional capacity to carry us into the heart of their world, though John was a far less exceptional person than Heloise, and his mind had none of Abelard's originality.

63

◄ 40 John of Salisbury likened a kingdom to a human body. This twelfth century diagram shows the common view of man as the microcosm of the four elements of which the world is composed, surrounded by the twelve winds

41 This chasuble, preserved at Sens where Becket spent part of his exile, is traditionally supposed to be his

42 Below, Henry II's tomb at Fontevrault

43 Right, Becket's murder, from a twelfth century manuscript – perhaps the earliest picture of it. It is followed by the text of John of Salisbury's letter 'Ex insperato . . .', the first written account

K inspato & in cosuu in
di gra ppitante nup
innotuit. qd ad uol e
rat lator psentiu tnsi
tur. Cautus g duuin
& munitiata occasione scbendi ad
amicu. ea gratu arripit. arbittus
in longe calamitatis magnu da

tolatiu. qd in tuis aurib; licea an
gratu cumulu deplorare. S; unde
sumet exordiu. Nam dicendi parit
inopia. matia copiosa & exubant.
& q uisi tepe nro malitia excreuis
set ad summu. fide excedit. Publica
angustias an domesticas deplora
bo? S; qualis mund agnouit. sua
queq; miseria punit acri. in forte

Thus John represents the humanism of the twelfth century in its two different senses: the love of the ancient world, and an interest in human emotions coupled with the capacity to express them. Latin letters were a characteristic milieu for the expression of this humanism. The genre had never entirely died between the days of Cicero or Pliny the Younger and the twelfth century; but it had been rare to find good Latin letters written and preserved, rarer still to find them in any measure expressive of their author's mind, between the fifth and the eleventh centuries. The eleventh century witnessed a notable revival, especially in Germany, and in the twelfth century, especially in France and England, letter writing flourished as an art.

John's most regular point of contact in England during his exile was in the chapter of Exeter cathedral, where his brother Richard of Salisbury lived with their mother and half-brother Robert, son of Egidia, under the kindly protection of Bishop Bartholomew, himself a noted theologian and canon lawyer, whom John had known at Paris and in Theobald's household. Bartholomew stayed openly loyal to the king, yet as time passed came more and more to lend his support to the archbishop; he represented the same coin as John, seen from a different side. The gift of a gold ring, set with a sapphire, with the inscription 'Christus vincit, Christus regnat, Christus imperat' – the acclamations used when kings and emperors were crowned – gave John the opportunity to unfold many aspects of his mind to his half-brother in a characteristic way, though it must be confessed that the metallurgy revealed is of a dubious character, in spite of John's boast that he had studied physics.

'Gold is incorruptible, abundant, expansive, can be diminished neither by fire nor by beating, is undefiled – it collects no rust, which makes it the guardian of other metals. Does gold not signify faith incorruptible; abundant, expansive charity; constancy in adverse circumstances; in prosperity temperance, preserver of the virtues ? . . . Roundness of shape is

44 'Cristus Vincit Cristus Reinat' on a sword made for Henry II's grandson, the Emperor Otto IV, c. 1200

a symbol of perfection, showing the sender to be perfect in the virtues aforesaid. The flash of a gem is the mirror of shining wisdom and knowledge.' And he goes on to torture mercilessly the symbolism of the sapphire and the meaning of the inscription. The link between the acclamations and kingship might have led him to Henry II; but this could have been dangerous to John, to Robert and to the bishop of Exeter; and so he adroitly turns to a theme which he had earlier developed: the wickedness of the Emperor Frederick Barbarossa, whose support for the anti-pope in the papal schism of 1159 and thereafter did so much to make Pope Alexander III's position weak and to foster his reluctance to take too firm a line with Henry II.

67

All this and more, which for brevity I pass over, I have observed in the ring, recognising in the gift a brother's love and instructed in many salutary ways to virtue by its quality. Is it not most just and right to love and cherish such a brother? Love is always permitted, never forbidden; and this I make and keep my theme ceaselessly and powerfully, so that I may joyfully give due worship to Love when I may. Meanwhile I thank you most warmly, asking you particularly to take care of our little brother and have a care too (so far as you may) for those who are attached to us.[12]

The use of symbolism, the high rhetoric, and expression of human friendship, of which the affection of man for man and especially of human brothers was the core, as a symbol of divine Love: all are characteristic of John and of the circle of humanists among whom he moved. Sometimes a lighter, sometimes a harsher note is struck. At some stage in his exile he learned that his old friend from Bishop Roger's circle and in the schools, Nicholas de Sigillo, had secured a plum in the game of patronage.[13] 'I seem to remember that there is a race of men known in the Church of God by the title archdeacons for whom you used to lament, my discerning friend, that every road to salvation was closed. They love gifts, you used to say, and follow after rewards; they are inclined to outrage, rejoice in false accusation, turn the sins of the people into food and drink, live by plunder so that a host is not safe with his guest. The most admirable of them preach the Law of God but do it not. Such and such like qualities your pious compassion used to bewail in the most wretched state of the men. Your friends, and all good men, must thank God and the bishop of Lincoln, who have opened your eyes and revealed to you a path by which this race of men can . . . attain salvation. . . .' For the bishop of Lincoln had appointed Nicholas to an archdeaconry in his diocese.

The exercises of the schools, and the range of John's learning and cast of mind, come out very clearly in a letter to his brother Richard.[14] He had written to the bishop of Exeter, yet had not felt able to speak his whole mind in a letter: sometimes he and his contemporaries overcame such a difficulty by sending verbal messages, sometimes (as was a common practice of John's) by sending a note to another friend in the same circle.

I had something to tell him, only the sheet of vellum was so small I had no space; and I want him to be convinced in my name, and would the Holy Spirit would convince him, who does not allow those who trust in Him to be without the comfort of his advice when in critical need. My point is this: I would that in this conflict of power and justice he march with such moderation, with law going before him, grace leading him by the hand, and reason in support, that he seem not guilty of rash folly against the power which God ordained[15] [Henry II], nor assent to wickedness to the injury of the Church, for fear of the power or love of transitory goods – and so be held not only to have forsaken his office, and violated his profession, but fought against justice, to the bane both of this generation and of posterity. Perhaps you will say that it is easier for me (as for everyone) to declare what is to be done by word than to perform it in deed. For the book which he is to eat is sweet in the prophet's mouth, but in his belly grows bitter.[16] The orator [Cicero] too in his *De inventione* teaches that to apply principles to an art or to discuss the art is easy, but to translate them out of art, that is, to practise what you preach, is very hard indeed. Nowhere is it harder than in the art of living, for that is the art of arts, and both for value and for difficulty beyond comparison exceeds all other arts. You will also add our comic poet's quip: 'when we are well we give sound advice to the sick; if you were in my case, you too would feel differently.'

My reply is: admitted that I have not known how to, and have not the capacity to keep this golden mean which I prescribe, nevertheless I will be so bold as to imitate the lyric poet who 'plays the whetstone's part, which can sharpen steel, but cannot cut itself'.

Instinct and education alike attracted John to the 'golden mean'; intellectually he came to call himself an *academicus*, a disciple of Aristotle and Cicero, in this sense: not a man lacking in principle, but a man who sought a middle way, a man who sat on the fence when there was no clear ground of principle on either side. He could be faint-hearted: early in his exile he despaired of effective support and told the archbishop to abandon canon law and take to prayer; on 29 December 1170, when the murderers broke into Canterbury Cathedral, he fled. But he hated to betray his principles or his friends, and when he saw his way clear, his sharpness of eye and command of the fluent, living Latin of his age produced a fine and sincere and eloquent utterance.

In 1166 Becket's strongest opponent among the bishops, Gilbert Foliot of London, succeeded in leading his colleagues in a general appeal against the archbishop and his works; their letter announcing the appeal was, as usual, passed on by Becket to John for his comments. John is at the heart of the matter without a moment's hesitation.[17] 'I have read with great care the letter which the children of the Church of Canterbury, your brothers and fellow-bishops, recently sent you, their father, for your consolation and the support of the Church after so long exile and proscription. My perusal suggested that nothing was more likely than that they were dictated by the counsel of Achitophel, who has evidently returned from Hell to plague the faithful, and written by the hand of Doeg the Edomite, still thirsting for the blood of the priests. . . .' Such labels were a common device to cover some particular enemy; and his identity is not long kept dark. 'Surely the bishop of London is he who first split the unity of the Church in England – as is known to all – and gripped by the ambition to be arch-bishop – as is suspected by most – was the first inspiration and inciter of the whole dispute ? Surely the very style of the letter reveals Achitophel and Doeg, of whose spirit it is full. . . . For his speech betrayeth him.'

JOHN AS HISTORIAN

Just as he had relieved his mind from the crisis of the 1150s by writing the *Policraticus*, so in the early part of his exile he set to work on another book, a history of recent events seen in relation to the papal court, the *Historia Pontificalis*. An interest in human affairs and in literary composition made the twelfth century something of a golden age in the writing of history; and it is as characteristic of the English contribution to the literature of the century that John should set his hand to historical writing as it is of its cosmopolitan nature that he should centre his story in the papal court. Literary historians of that age either reveal themselves to be primarily interested in reconstructing the past or in narrating the events of their own day. William of Malmesbury, writing in the tradition of the Venerable Bede, was a master of the art of reconstruction – though no mean narrator, too, of contemporary affairs. Eadmer, monk of Canterbury and biographer of St Anselm, cared only for the history of recent events (see p. 168). John walked in Eadmer's footsteps, and his history evaded the period between the Flood and the author's lifetime, which most chroniclers felt conscientiously bound to sketch in, by pretend-ing to be a continuation of a continuation of a well-known continental chronicle with which it had no conceivable connection – save that it happened to end in the year of grace 1148, when John's close links with the papal court began.

What survives is a marvellous fragment, often vivid and pungent, often revealing John's curious gift of appearing to say more than he does. It opens with an account of the papal council at Rheims in 1148, which occupies over a third of the book.[18] He makes a bow to one characteristic interest, the privileges of the see of Canterbury, then devotes most of the space to the intrigues of St Bernard and his attempt to secure the condemnation of the now ageing, subtle, obscure theologian and bishop of Poitiers, Gilbert de la Porrée. This battle of giants is portrayed with delicate irony, so that neither side is shown to have a victory, and neither suffers real defeat. He observes that some condemned Bernard for his successful attack on Abelard and his unsuccessful attack on Gilbert de la Porrée; but John for his part reckons that so holy a man must have based his case on God's zeal; and that Bishop Gilbert's argument, though it seemed totally obscure to very many, must have made sense. By these gentle pricks John reconciled the formidable contestants after their deaths; then proceeded to describe their tactics, culminating in Bernard's discomfiture. At this point John's own involvement is revealed: 'I recall that I myself approached the bishop on the abbot's behalf and requested a meeting in any religious house in Poitou, in France [i.e. the Île de France] or in Burgundy, of the bishop's selection, so that they could have a friendly conference, without disputation, on the sayings of St Hilary' – out of which Gilbert had confuted Bernard. 'The bishop replied that it was sufficient that they had disputed thus far; and that if the abbot wished to understand Hilary fully, he should first take a course in the liberal arts and other essential prolegomena to knowledge.'

Later in the book he gives the famous picture of Henry of Blois, bishop of Winchester, one of the most intriguing and tantalizing figures of the period. We can get a glimpse through many windows into his personality, but never more than a glimpse. He was a Cluniac monk with a lifelong devotion to his monastery, to which he returned whenever his political troubles made a period of sabbatical leave desirable; it seems clear that he loved both the regularity and the panache of Cluny. His uncle, King Henry I of England, endowed him as a prince: he combined one of the richest sees, Winchester, with one of the richest abbeys in England, Glastonbury. A little snatch of autobiography among the Glastonbury records reveals a man who loved the waving corn and all the details of estate management, and helps us to understand Henry the eminent financier. An inventory of the treasures of Winchester cathedral which he gave or redeemed from pawn reveals the Cluniac patron – and to John's story of his search for old statues in Rome we shall return anon. What figures most in John's pages are Henry's involvement in politics and his intrigues against Archbishop Theobald, John's old lord and master.

Henry was believed to be instigating his brother the king [Stephen] against the church, though indeed the king took advice neither from him nor from any man of wisdom, as his actions plainly show. It chanced meanwhile that the king oppressed the church with fresh persecutions, and when the news was brought to the pope the bishop of Winchester, who happened to be with him, exclaimed: 'How glad I am that I am not there now, or this persecution would be laid at my door.' Smiling, the pope gave tongue to the following fable: 'The devil and his dam were chatting to each other, as friends do, and whilst she was endeavouring to curb her son's evil-doing by rebuking him and chiding him for his misdeeds, a storm arose in their sight and many ships were sunk. "See," said the devil, "if I had been there you would have blamed me for this mischief." Said she, "Even if you were not actually on the spot, you have certainly trailed your tail there beforehand."' And turning the moral against the bishop, he added, 'Ask yourself, my brother, if you have not been trailing *your* tail in the English sea.'

Count Hugh, a Norman from Apulia, came to the same pope, the Cistercian Eugenius III, demanding a divorce, or, as we should say, annulment of his marriage. The pope first investigated the case, and then dismissed his witnesses as unsuitable. Finally he confirmed the marriage: 'And then, his face covered with tears, he leapt down from his throne, in the sight of all, great man though he was, and lay at the feet of the count, so that his mitre rolled in the dust and was found between the feet of the astounded count after the bishops and cardinals had lifted the pope up.' In a highly emotional scene the pope urged the count to take back his wife; gave her to him indeed with a ring of his own, and 'invested' the count with the lady; and John duly notes that he was an eye-witness. It seems that the reconciliation was a temporary affair; but even if he failed, the pope's attitude and his manner of work are important, for they reveal the human interest lying behind the legal tangles of the papal court and the papal decretals.

Shortly before these events, the law of the Church on marriage and on every other topic under the sun had been investigated in a great book written by Master Gratian of Bologna. To Gratian and canon law we must now turn; but not before we have observed that besides his humanism, his philosophic calm and his skill as a writer, it remains significant that John of Salisbury was present at the papal court on this occasion. For he was also an expert on appeals to Rome and a practising canon lawyer. The mixture is characteristic of the unspecialized nature of learning in the first half of the twelfth century; and of the mixture of interests of English scholars of this age. The renaissance was a cosmopolitan movement: John visited Paris and Rheims, the courts of France and Rome; his own comrades in the circle of the Norman archbishop of Canterbury included Italians as well as Englishmen. The interest in history and canon law was perhaps especially common among the English; and John, whose life was spent in Paris and Rheims and Rome and Chartres, speaks in his letters as if he never quite felt at home outside England. Yet he was a cosmopolitan scholar first and foremost, and a moving witness to the community of minds among the Latin-writing, Latin-speaking clergy of the renaissance.

IV MASTER GRATIAN OF BOLOGNA

A baffling obscurity surrounds the author of the *Concord of Discordant Canons*. No book influenced the twelfth century schools more profoundly; and not the schools only, for it laid the foundation both of the science and of the practice of canon law, and so of the shape of papal monarchy, for centuries to come. Yet that highly articulate age spared hardly a word for Gratian himself. The most reliable tradition tells us something entirely unexpected: that he was neither a teacher nor a practising lawyer, but a recluse, a monk of the enclosed order of Camaldoli, living in Bologna, the centre of legal studies, yet apart from the world. But on closer inspection this becomes intelligible, even essential to the understanding of the book.

We have likened him already to Adam Smith, who revolutionized the study of economics in part for the very reason that he was neither a practising economist nor a city man, but a philosopher by training, able to view the science with fresh eyes, and to see it whole. In Gratian's early years learning was not so specialized as it later became. In particular, theology and canon law, the higher disciplines of the schools, were not divided. It is true that theology came in the early twelfth century to be particularly associated with Paris, law with Bologna; but in neither city were the schools exclusive, nor were they the only centres, by a very long way, for these particular sciences. It is clear that Gratian had absorbed much of what his world had to offer in both theology and law, and it may be that he had visited Paris as a young man; he had certainly sat at Abelard's feet in the spirit if not in the flesh. Equally certainly, he knew what was stirring in Bologna's

75

schools, though to the practice of her courts he seems to have been serenely indifferent.

The schools of the north grew where a great teacher held forth; but they were clerical schools, controlled by the Church, peopled by 'clerks'; and a clerk was a clergyman in that age, not necessarily in orders, but at least tonsured – his head had been shaven to mark him off from the laity. In Italy there was no such distinction: laymen went to school as well as clerics; the tradition of learning often had its centre in a law school, and the law students and the lawyers were as often laymen as clergy. The law they practised derived ultimately from the law of the late Roman Empire, but down to the eleventh century its practitioners knew little of the major source books of Roman law, and much of what they practised would have seemed strange and unfamiliar to Ulpian or Papinian. In the eleventh century a revival of legal learning began, with its centre in Pavia and Bologna; and the credit for the final recovery of the whole *Corpus Juris Civilis* of Justinian belongs to a Bolognese lawyer of the late eleventh century, even more obscure than Gratian, called Irnerius.

This was one of the most important events of the twelfth century renaissance; for it revealed to a small but astonished audience not only a compilation on the largest scale of all authorities for a system of law, but a world of thought which interpreted and harmonized and made intelligible this whole, vast, impressive system. It revealed, in a word, the idea of system in a way that was wholly new in that age. The *Corpus* is a considerable mouthful, and it is doubtful whether many outside the law schools of the north Italian cities really attempted to master it in the twelfth century; copies of it in northern Europe of that period are rare. None the less its influence was profound, in many intellectual spheres and in several legal systems.

The idea of arranging the authorities of the church's law in intelligible order was nothing new in the early twelfth century. A century before, Bishop Burchard of Worms had put together a useful manual of the main authorities in a rational scheme. At the turn of the eleventh and twelfth centuries, Ivo of Chartres had made both a large compilation and a smaller introductory manual; and Ivo was in some measure at least influenced by Roman law in his search for system and his choice of materials. Not for the first time items of Roman law passed muster in his collection as authorities for canon law, where the writings of popes and councils and the fathers of the Church failed to solve a particular problem. Gratian's attitude to Roman law was ambivalent. Its theory profoundly influenced him; its practice he rejected. He was not a great textual scholar, and there are obvious mistakes in his texts; none the less, the compilation is far fuller than any earlier one, and this in itself was a notable achievement. Even more remarkable is the assumption, consistently and ruthlessly carried through, that it is possible to view the whole of this inchoate mass as a series of intelligible, flowing arguments. In part both these achievements reflect the influence upon him of Justinian's *Corpus*. But Roman law as an authority he repudiated. In the *Concordia* – or the *Decretum*, to give it the name by which it has usually been known – as it circulated in the middle of the twelfth century, there are a number of texts from Roman law. But it has been shown that these were not part of

46 Ivo of Chartres; a twelfth century copy of his introductory manual of canon law, the *Panormia*: 'Incipit prologus Panormic Ivonis Carnotensis episcopi'

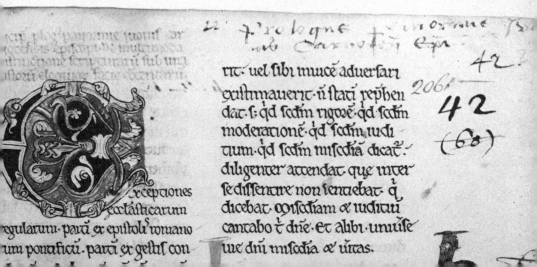

Gratian's original design. Their exclusion had the curious consequence that the book as originally written provided a large framework of principle, and solutions to innumerable difficulties; but almost no guidance as to how to resolve these difficulties in practice. Canon law was an ancient system in its own right, but its courts had never been properly organized; many of its rules were highly sophisticated already; its procedure (on paper at any rate) was primitive and unformed. To fill this gap, the natural inclination of twelfth century churchmen was to look to Roman law, and from Roman law and their own experience the gap was rapidly filled. And so Gratian's disciples infiltrated a number of texts after his own work was finished, and the fact that this was necessary underlines two striking features of his work: its academic inspiration, and Gratian's passionate involvement in the contest of empire and papacy.

Ivo's books, and especially his famous preface, had provided the inspiration of Abelard's *Sic et non*. For a moment, Abelard put theology ahead of canon law in the scientific race. Although he may not have read the *Sic et non* Gratian, in effect, showed that he had grasped Abelard's message; and this fact is all the more striking in that he may well have been of an age with Abelard. Between the day, in or about 1140, when the *Decretum* was finished, and the moment a decade later when Peter the Lombard finished his *Sentences*, law was ahead of theology once again. So close were the links between the two studies that such a situation could not last; that it happened at all in the age of Abelard is a measure of Gratian's achievement. His is, indeed, a thoroughly academic work. For the most part, it is the exigencies of a continuous, flowing argument which dictate its arrangement, and it is peculiarly difficult for a modern reader to find his way about it. The difficulty did not arise for early students, since they expected to learn their way about a labyrinth of this kind, and they filled its margins with glosses, including a handsome number of cross references. Here is a sample of his method.

The *Decretum* falls into three parts, of which the second and largest consists of a series of *Causae*, imaginary cases, used as a frame for asking critical legal questions, which are then answered by citation of authorities and by Gratian's own comments, the 'dicta Gratiani'. Two of the *Causae* on marriage (C.28, 29) open in the following fashion.

A married infidel was converted to the faith; but his wife, owing to her hatred for the Christian faith, deserted him. He took a Christian lady to wife, and when she died became a clerk. At length, because of the virtue of his life and his learning, he was elected a bishop. The first question (*Quaestio* 1) is whether there can be true marriage between infidels? The second, whether it was lawful for this man to marry a second wife while the first lived? The third, whether a man should be deemed a bigamist who marries one wife before, another after baptism?

Gratian's final answer to each question seems somewhat surprising today: between infidels there can be honourable marriage, but it cannot be binding; if an infidel wife, married while both were infidels, deserts her husband, he (even though now a Christian) may marry again; but if he does so, he is technically a 'bigamist' – in the medieval sense, of a man who has married twice, not of a man who has two wives – and this was reckoned a bar to higher orders. Even though St Jerome allowed it, St Augustine clearly repudiated the idea that the man of this imaginary *Causa* could be a bishop; and Gratian, following Augustine and Pope Innocent I, rejected his election. He passed on to a set of contingencies (to a modern audience) equally remote.

News came to a noble lady that a certain nobleman's son sought her for wife. Another man, not of noble, indeed of servile, origin . . . pretended to be the suitor, and duly took her to wife; she gave her consent. The first suitor . . . came

79

at last and also sought her to be his wife. She complained that she had been deceived, and wished to marry the first man who wooed her. The first question is, whether she was truly married to the second suitor? The second, if she first thought he was a free man, then discovered he was a slave, whether she can leave him on this ground?

The former question inspired Gratian to a whole flight of subtle distinctions; but the essence of the matter was that if a man 'was thought to be Virgil, and he turned out to be Plato', then an *error personae* had occurred; and if a woman consented to one man and was deceived into marrying another, she could not be said to have given her consent, which Gratian accepted as essential for a valid marriage, and so she was free. As to the slave, the authorities were clear: anyone can marry a slave, and in the eyes of God this is a valid and binding marriage; but if he or she was not known to be a slave, then the other partner is free. This *Quaestio* opens with St Paul's great saying that in Christ 'There is neither Jew nor Greek, there is neither bond nor free' – *ergo*, says Gratian, it must be the same in the marriage of Christians. But however it might be in Christ, in medieval society, especially in southern Europe, bond and free were not in all respects of one condition.

One of Gratian's authorities was a passage from Justinian's *Code*, which was masquerading under the label 'Pope Julius', and so evaded his efforts to exclude Roman law. Usually he was more successful; and his own personal reason for breaking with current tradition in this way seems to have been his personal antagonism for the empire – and so for legal sources depending on the authority of Roman emperors – and his devotion to the papacy. The papacy was generally accepted as the supreme appeal court in Christendom. But it was only about the time that the book was issued that appeals to the papacy came to be a normal part of the life of the Church. From this point of view it was peculiarly well timed. For a host of reasons litigants were finding it convenient to carry cases to

47 The Law of Marriage. This illustrates another problem involving 'bigamy' – whether a lady whose betrothed had taken religious vows is free to marry another; from a twelfth century copy of Gratian, *Causa 27* ▶

castitatis habens desponsauit sibi u
xorem. Iua priori condicioni renun
tians transtulit se ad alium: illi nup
sit. Iue cui prius desponsata fuit repe
tit eam. Hic primum queritur an
coniugium possit ee. int̃ uouentes.
Scdo an liceat sponse á sponso disce
dere: 7 alii nubere. Quod uero uo
uentes matrimonia contrahere non
possint multis auctoritatib; pbatur.

De uo_
9 an possit

Rome on appeal. What was needed was a code of law, and a system of courts with a procedure sufficiently sophisticated to meet the new demands. As a compilation of authorities based firmly on the principle that in all matters of spiritual law the papacy was supreme, Gratian in great measure met the first need. As a basic compilation, his book remained the foundation of canonical studies down to the twentieth century. It could not strictly be an official compilation, since it contained a great deal of private speculation by its author, to which the papacy never lent its authority. But it was soon accepted at Rome as the basic source book; and its status was canonized when the first official collection of papal decretals, the *Decretals* of Pope Gregory IX of 1234, were issued as a supplement to it.

In two ways Gratian particularly stimulated the study as well as the practice of law. His compilation revealed, in many cases for the first time, just where the gaps were and just where the major problems lay; and his own solutions were in many cases so preposterous as to stimulate younger students to disagree with him and put him right.

The development of appeals to Rome is fairly obscure; but a window is opened at an early stage in the letters John of Salisbury wrote as archbishop's secretary in the late 1150s. Many of them deal with surprisingly trivial cases, revealing the rapidity with which the idea had taken root among clerical litigants in distant parts of Europe, but also the crucial difficulties of this stage in the development of the law. The definition of the rights of parishes and parish priests and the nature of parish boundaries – of rights to tithes and burial dues and the like – created a host of problems, and not merely material problems, in a Church keenly aware of the need to develop and stabilize pastoral care in parishes. These are the commonest themes of the disputes recorded in John's letters. But canon law also ruled issues profoundly affecting secular society. The outstanding case in John's letters is the famous suit of Richard of Anstey, the 'immortal plaintiff' as Maitland called him, who successfully sued for his uncle's inheritance on the ground that his cousin, his uncle's heiress, was illegitimate. The inheritance was a matter for the royal court, but the royal court was no less strict than the Church's courts on the principle of legitimate succession, and this depended on the law of marriage, which was a matter for the courts spiritual, presided over by archdeacons, bishops, archbishops and, finally, the pope: and to the archbishop's court Richard's case went eighteen times, and to the pope's, twice. In the process, his uncle's tenants in and around Essex were made to feel the presence of the papal monarchy in their midst: for the facts of a tangled case could not be elicited in Rome, and according to the normal process the pope delegated the investigation to 'judges delegate' – in this case a bishop and an abbot – in England, himself determining the issue in law.

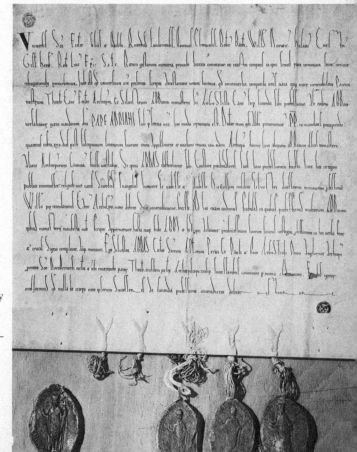

48 Papal judges delegate. The bishops of London, Evreux, Bath, Norwich, Chichester, Hereford and Lincoln – a galaxy of bishops for a major case – act as delegates of Pope Adrian IV. Four of the seven seals survive – those of London, Bath(?), Chichester and Hereford

Marriage in the twelfth century was a very unstable institution, partly because the hazards of life were such as to make the early death of one or other partner a common event, partly because of the tangle of marriage law. In principle divorce in the modern sense was forbidden; but bishops and popes were well aware that customs and practices were very various; that the law was uncertain, and doctrine itself unstable. The pope who settled the Anstey affair, Alexander III (1159–81), was himself an eminent theologian and canonist, a Bolognese disciple of Gratian with great practical experience of legal cases and ecclesiastical administration. Yet he changed his mind several times as to what constituted a valid marriage. He wished to say that it should take place in church, or at least before a priest, so that its sacramental character could be recognized, and the nature of the witness needed clearly defined.

He soon found that to enforce such a rule would annul a great proportion of the marriages in Christendom. Marriage seems normally to have been entered by processes more informal than we should readily believe. But not by haphazard. In high society it had come to be seen as the key to the passage of landed property, and this was made its central purpose, to which all else was subordinated. This had the effect of making the secular aristocracy take marriage and legitimacy much more seriously at a time when the Church was erecting it into a sacrament. Theologians were in the paradoxical position of emphasizing the sacred character of a union, much of whose purpose lay in the marriage bed and its consequences, while clinging to an old ascetic doctrine that carnal pleasure must contain an element of sin. Yet for all this Pope Alexander's view of marriage was in certain respects considerably more humane than that of the secular aristocracy.

The earl of Oxford, for example, became affianced to the young daughter of a royal chamberlain. Before the marriage

84

49 Marriage as the key to the passage of landed property. A lord transmits feudal rights by giving his daughter in marriage with his wife's approval; from a Spanish manuscript of the late twelfth century ▶

could be consummated, the chamberlain fell into disgrace, and forfeited his lands. She was no longer an heiress, and in the earl's eyes, no longer marriageable. But the lady, though very young and at his mercy, announced in a most determined way that he had given her his promise in such form that their marriage could not be broken. The earl imprisoned her and subjected her to every kind of contumely to compel her to drop her claim; while giving the most unchivalrous reasons why the marriage could not go on. But her complaint came to the ears of the bishop and the pope, and they could not ignore her. By now the dispute between Thomas Becket and Henry II was at its height, and pope and bishop were reluctant to force an issue so delicate, so near the heart of the social customs and assumptions of Henry's court. So the lady's lamentations passed almost unheeded for six or seven years. Then Becket's murder changed the situation, the pope ordered an investigation, and made a peremptory judgment. The earl submitted, and twenty years of married life, outwardly successful, and several children, followed.

A deeper understanding of the nature of Christian marriage was shown by Heloise and Abelard fifty years before. It is indeed a strange irony that the union of an eminent celibate cleric and his mistress should reveal a deeper understanding of the issues than the best minds of the next generation could muster. Yet it is of such ironies that history is made.

The paradox is very deep indeed. Every line in Heloise's letters reveals the depth of her devotion to Abelard. Their purpose, it is true, was to bring home to him her dependence; yet their sincerity is abundantly clear, and is confirmed by the extraordinary passage in his own *Historia* in which he describes at length her arguments against marriage. Heloise tells us, in effect, that her religious vocation was solely on Abelard's account, that the central experience of her life was her devotion to him, and that she was an abbess out of obedience to Abelard, not to any divine vocation. Her devotion was so complete that she preferred to be his mistress to being his wife. According to his account, she had three grounds for dissuading him from marriage: that it would by no means placate the anger of her uncle; that married life, the milling throng of children, was no context for the true life of a philosopher; that the disgrace of falling victim to it would destroy his career. In Heloise's letters we can see the clear reflection of two quite different worlds of ideas: the traditional world of the cathedral close, in which marriage is illegal but common, and informal relations between the sexes quite normal; and the world of the papal reform and the new theological movements, in which marriage is a sacrament, blessed by the Church, in which the two partners themselves can live the sacrament together – but from which canons and clergy and theologians are excluded by the special nature of their profession. As the law then stood, it was illegal for Abelard to marry, since he was a canon of Sens cathedral, and probably also in higher orders.[19] But as the law then stood the marriage was valid: once entered, the marriage bond tied them and could only be unravelled by both parties entering religious houses. The ceremony took place in church, as most, apparently, did not; but it was secret, and the couple lived apart after their union. The tragedy of Heloise was that she could see in the mind of the great theologian, whose love consumed her, a vision of Christian marriage more intense and lofty than conventional theologians approached for many centuries to come, but which their circumstances forbade them to live.

The theologians and lawyers of the twelfth century struggled as best they might with the tangle of marriage customs. After Pope Alexander III had abandoned the position that a valid marriage must take place in church, he still faced the difficult problems whether formal consent alone in the presence of witnesses was sufficient for a marriage, or whether more was needed; whether, as Master Gratian had taught, consummation was essential to make a marriage binding. In the end he concluded that if the words of consent clearly indicated the will to take a partner there and then, a binding marriage contract was made. In many of their letters we can see the popes of the late twelfth and early thirteenth centuries striving to make some sort of humane and reasonable sense out of a multiplicity of circumstances and cases; and their decisions willy nilly affected every stratum of society. In this field Gratian had attempted to propound practical solutions; and it was one of many where his efforts provided a foundation on which the more sophisticated legal minds of the second half of the twelfth century could build more subtle, yet soundly constructed, systems of law. They can hardly be blamed if the marriage law of the century touched only the fringe of the problem to which it was directed. St Paul had likened the union of husband

MARRIAGE HUMAN AND DIVINE

50 Jesus at the marriage of Cana ('in Chana Galilee')

51 Family life in the Reuner Musterbuch (see p. 26)

and wife to that of Christ and the Church; but all the richness of teaching about human and divine love in the twelfth century was rarely applied by theologians to their doctrine of marriage. Human love took on new meaning in the hands of John of Salisbury and St Bernard; but it meant simply sincere, warm human friendship, between man and man. The vernacular writers of the late twelfth century have much to say of human love; but many of them saw, or pretended to see, no link between love and marriage. In this, as in so much else, the legal renaissance which Gratian led was a brilliant pioneering effort; but it was not, as some have thought it, the key to unlock the chains which bound twelfth century society.

52 The marriage of Christ and the Church; from a twelfth century copy of Bede's Commentary on the Song of Songs

THE PERIOD: ROMANESQUE AND GOTHIC

In the history of art and architecture, the period of this book, the late eleventh and twelfth centuries, is in some respects convenient, in some wholly confusing. This is what we should expect. The concept of the 'renaissance' was devised by historians of ideas: between the growth of new ideas, the development of education, the sophistication of minds, and the craftsmanship of the day there was naturally some relation; where this relation is most effective, the period has meaning. In certain respects, however, craftsmanship developed according to a different rhythm from that of the schools. This means that in a small book no effort can be made to describe the story of art and architecture in general – even in the most superficial way; there must be a concentration on those points where art, society and ideas met.

The centuries from the ninth to the twelfth were the ages of Carolingian, Ottonian and Romanesque architecture and art; and Romanesque (tenth–twelfth centuries) is now commonly divided into 'first' and 'second'.[20] The twelfth century saw the rise of Gothic, first visible in Abbot Suger's Saint-Denis, only finally conquering earlier taste and custom in the thirteenth century. 'Romanesque', the massive style especially associated at its height with solid churches distantly based on Roman basilicas, was the idiom in which the architects of the tenth and eleventh centuries developed their enormous churches and cathedrals, on a scale far beyond that normal for many centuries before; first in the Germany of the Ottos, then in France and southern Europe, finally, after the Norman Conquest, in England too. In the art of painting, as in architecture, there is a marked difference between the dominant centres: between Germany, where new techniques of painting, and especially a new deployment of brilliant colour, grew up under the shadow of the great basilicas; and England, where a more modest old-fashioned architectural tradition survived, alongside which a brilliant style of painting grew, the 'Winchester school' of the tenth and eleventh centuries, with luxuriant leafy scrolls and figures in draperies which flutter eternally. This was closely associated with a tradition of line drawing of great vitality, different from the tradition of German art, even though both ultimately derived from a common, Carolingian, source. All over Europe, throughout the early and central Middle Ages, one finds artists and architects taking occasional note of an obvious 'authority', a piece of Roman building or sculpture; and one finds now and then the impress of Byzantine influence. One also finds many local variations and local styles, sometimes reflecting the vitality of a group of notable craftsmen, sometimes mere isolation from the currents of the world. But in several parts of Europe the late eleventh and early twelfth centuries saw some marked changes, which were partly technological, partly artistic. The development of the stone vault in such places as Caen and Durham prepared for the immense heights of Gothic cathedrals. The art of glass painting was no novelty; but the idea of providing churches with permanent sets of stained glass windows only became at all widespread in this age. At the same time the idea of adorning churches with large schemes of sculpture was revived, and the plainness of old Romanesque was converted into the richness of new. This was largely a matter of fashion; but it was helped in the early twelfth century by the revival of chisels suited to deep under-cutting, the weapons which made possible the supreme achievements of Romanesque sculpture in France. The old pattern of local styles and wider influences was a kaleidoscope, and in this period the kaleidoscope took several turns. Such a turn was the rapid transformation of England, after the Norman Conquest, from the home of conservative architectural traditions, in one

53 'One of the Roman gate-
ways still surviving at Autun,
known as the Porte
d'Arroux, must have been
well known to the builders of
Romanesque churches in
Burgundy' (D. Grivot and
G. Zarnecki, *Gislebertus,
Sculptor of Autun*, p. 19)

54 The pointed arches and
fluted pilasters of the nave of
Autun cathedral were to be
found in its chief model at
Cluny; but the small arcade
above the great arches
reminds us of the Porte
d'Arroux, which also has
fluted pilasters

of the most dramatic building explosions in the recorded history of under-developed countries. In painting the Norman Conquest had no such immediate effect. The English had taught the Normans to paint before the Conquest and still did so after; they were already part of a single world before the wind changed and blew William the Conqueror across the Channel in September 1066. It was in part, however, the natural link between the Norman empire in Sicily and in England which explains the powerful flow of Byzantine influence in the early twelfth century: in the St Albans Psalter one sees the birth of a new style in which German colour and Byzantine form are more evident than earlier English traditions; a style especially characteristic of this country, but in its birth evidence of the cosmopolitan nature of twelfth century art.

Imitation of Roman remains can be found in every age, especially in southern Europe; but it received a new impetus in the twelfth century. Yet there is a sense in which the rise of Gothic involved a flight from Rome. In Autun cathedral one may see all these tendencies in one building: the technological achievements in the lofty stone vault and the deep chiselling of the sculpture; Romanesque tradition in the survival of round-headed arches and the massive size and weight of the building; Roman influence in the direct imitation of a Roman arch outside the city; the new Gothic idiom in the extensive use (even in so Roman and Romanesque a setting) of the pointed arch, which may owe something to technological need, but may well also reflect – via its immediate model, the great abbey church of Cluny – the meeting of western masons and patrons with the masons and the architecture of Islam (see pp. 117 ff.).

THE THEME: PATRON, BUILDER AND ARTIST

There is here a rich profusion of problems; to make any sense of them one must find a clear path through the forest – though at the risk of making the creative energy of the eleventh and twelfth centuries appear much simpler and cruder than it was.

55 Durham cathedral: the nave, with massive Romanesque arches and the great vault of the 1120s, supported on pointed arches

In this chapter I want to ask a simple question: when we look at a twelfth century cathedral or abbey, whether we look at the overall effect of the architecture or the minute and complex detail of ornament, sculpture and glass painting, are we looking into the minds of illiterate craftsmen who developed their own traditions step by step? – or of educated bishops, canons and monks, who directed the schemes from their own knowledge of other work in progress at the time, or related it to theological ideas, to elements in fashion and religious sentiment, of their own choosing?

Norman building in England reached its zenith in buildings like Durham cathedral, one of the most complete expressions of Romanesque architecture, with massive columns, heavy,

56 Saint-Denis: Suger's ambulatory, the cradle of Gothic, with pointed arches supported on Suger's columns (see pp. 129–32)

semi-circular arches and bold ornament. Yet already there were signs of a change of style: the nave vaults of the 1120s mark a technical advance which showed the way for the founders of Gothic architecture to build the enormously lofty vaults of the French cathedrals; and while the Durham masons were completing their task the masons of Saint-Denis, just outside Paris, under the direction of Abbot Suger, were beginning to think of developing the pointed arch (already adumbrated at Durham and Cluny[21]), the lighter, brighter, and loftier genius of Gothic. The change took time, and the terms Romanesque and Gothic can confuse us as to its nature and aims. But there is no doubt that it heralded the major change in the technique and fashion of building of the twelfth century.

57 The east end of Speyer
cathedral illustrates the massive,
simple grandeur of a great
German cathedral of the
eleventh–twelfth centuries

58 Vézelay abbey in Burgundy:
Christ and the apostles preside
over the tympanum above the
west door, and the vista of a vast
church of the early twelfth
century opens at their feet

The city of Durham was well designed by nature to be a
fortress and a refuge against the attacks of the marauding
Scots; and the Normans developed it in a substantial and
characteristic way, by building a large castle and a huge
cathedral, occupying a considerable part of the area. Similarly,
a smaller cathedral and a smaller castle occupied a great part
of the site of John of Salisbury's home town, and we can still
walk over the site and see how little was left for mortal habi-
tation when God and Caesar had had their share.

The size of the great cathedrals reflects their function and
the fashion of the age. The fashion for building vast churches
grew in Germany in the tenth century, and in the eleventh
spread everywhere in western Europe, most conspicuously to

96

northern and central France and, with the Normans, into England. But the increasing size of their east ends also reflected the need for space for growing ritual in the liturgy, and for growing numbers of monks or canons; and the increasing size of their naves reflected the expectation that on great festivals the layfolk of Durham and the country round would come in throngs to worship at the shrine of St Cuthbert and join in the solemnity of High Mass; on the feast of Pentecost the Norman bishops expected the parish priests from every corner of the diocese to lead a fair number of their layfolk to pay court to the bishop and the cathedral and pay their respects in prayers and in cash. Their size also reflects, perhaps, the love of the age for flowing processions. Thus, briefly and crudely, the two

97

types of inspiration twelfth century design might have were fashion and function; the definition of these will, I hope, become a little less crude as we proceed.

In the building of churches in the Middle Ages there was always likely to be a union of minds between patron and architect more intimate than we are accustomed to see. First of all, the architect, or master mason, was not an occasional visitor but the constant director of the operation, contractor and manager as well as architect. In the conditions of the time the architect of a major project, say, in a monastery, might be living in the monastery for years at a time, and this would naturally involve the constant exchange of views and explanations from both sides of their aims and problems. Again, medieval architecture was in large measure a traditional architecture. Buildings which departed radically from existing norms or from models of some kind were comparatively rare; direct imitation was very common; new ideas frequently came by imitation of distant or ancient buildings. Thus the patron's instruction was often more closely related to the finished

59 February in the calendar of the St Albans Psalter, c. 1120 (see pp. 144 ff.)

Febroarl haber dics̄ xxvm· &lunã
xx· ix· 7 in bisō̄· dics̄ xx· ix· lun· xxx·
Quarta subir mortem·
prosternir tercia fortem·

D̄ KE̅ sap̄. Sc̄e Brigide virginis.

product than would be the case today. For good and ill a modern building committee does not normally brief an architect – would not dare to brief an architect – on design or style; it briefs him on function, needs and so forth, and then says its prayers while he is at the drawing board. In this respect one must accept the unfashionable opinion that the Gothic revival of the nineteenth century was nearer in spirit to the Middle Ages than we are. One can point to countless medieval buildings of real artistic originality. But one can also point to stories like that of the German Cistercian community of the early thirteenth century which sent a lay brother to France to make drawings of Clairvaux abbey so that its buildings could be precisely reproduced in their own enclosure; and more immediate to our purpose, when Waterhouse, in the 1860s, took as his model a bay from a French château and repeated it many times to form his new building at Gonville and Caius College, Cambridge, he was doing much what the architect of Autun cathedral did in making a Roman arch in the city his model and repeating it numerous times to make a triforium arcade.

60 Gilbert's February on the west door of Autun cathedral, c. 1125–35 (see p. 117 ff.)

61 February in the calendar on the west front of Amiens cathedral, c. 1230

The third and most substantial reason why patron and architect were closer in the Middle Ages than now, is that the greater churches in particular represented, and in their wall-painting, glass and sculpture directly portrayed, large symbolic and iconographic schemes. It is clear that the iconography was in the main dictated by the patrons, as indeed was the case in fifteenth century Italy; but this is not to say that the artists were always ignorant of the sources from which the iconography derived or incapable of having their own ideas. In many instances, the patrons may have accepted schemes or ideas – for groups of ideas are far more common than uniform schemes covering a whole building – which were proposed to them. To take one example, it is unlikely that the sculptor of the exquisite font at Liège had direct access to the writings of Rupert of Deutz, or a similar contemporary interpreter, on whom its symbolism is closely based, as well as to the classical sculpture which palpably inspired the craftsman's style. In a similar way the peculiar geometry which underlies so much Gothic architecture, and the mathematics of proportion, must have started their life in the minds of educated mathematicians.

62 The bronze font at Liège, 1107–18, showing the baptism of Jesus, and resting on twelve oxen, like the metal bowl in Solomon's Temple. These are elements in an elaborate symbolism based on the Old and New Testaments as interpreted in the twelfth century

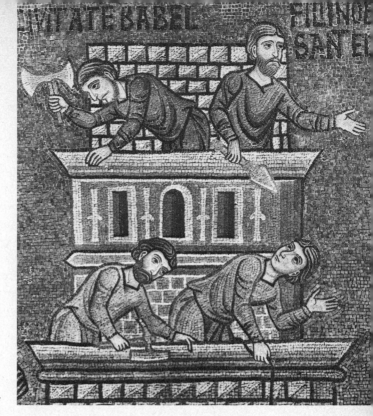

63 Masons at work on the
Tower of Babel in a mosaic
in the Palatine chapel in
Palermo, mid-twelfth century

A CRUCIAL CASE: THE ORIGINS OF GOTHIC

The switch from Romanesque to Gothic is marked by technological advance, by new elements of style, and by a new
relationship between geometry and proportions. It used to be
thought that the essence of the change was the introduction of
the pointed arch, and that this was due to Moslem influence.
In recent generations other sources for the pointed arch –
Romanesque interlace and the exigencies of vaulting – have
been pointed out; and the current fashion is to see the inspiration
of Gothic in technological achievement, most specifically in
the capacity to build lofty vaults and the development of stained
glass windows, without which the characteristic combination
of great height and coloured lights which one can still appreciate, on a sunny day at a cathedral like Chartres, could not

101

be achieved. Very recently, Mr John Harvey has revived the unfashionable idea that the pointed arch lies at the heart of the change, observing very justly that it is the element of design most conspicuous to patrons not versed in the subtleties of vault technology, and that the shape of the pointed arches is invariably a vital element in the stylistic effect of major Gothic buildings.[22] Clearly, the story is complex; yet one may well feel that Mr Harvey is right to draw our attention once again to Moslem inspiration. This he does in two ways: first, by showing that the kind of pointed arch which became so conspicuous in western Europe could not readily be found in parts of Islam normally accessible to the west, but in parts of Syria and Turkey opened up by the First Crusade. If there was direct influence from these areas, it must have been due to the observation of knights and ecclesiastics who visited the crusading kingdoms, and also to the experience of trained masons capable of transporting the vital elements of design – most probably, perhaps, by the transmission of Moslem masons to the west. Secondly, he points out the coincidence between the increased precision of geometrical knowledge and ideas – both in craftsmanship, be it said, and in the use of symbolic schemes

MOSLEM INFLUENCE
ON GOTHIC
ARCHITECTURE

64 The arcade of the Great Mosque at Diyarbakir in south-east Turkey, 1117–25; from a photograph by Mr John Harvey

– and the revival of Euclid. Euclid's *Elements* were first introduced into medieval Christendom by Adelard of Bath, the most voracious collector of ancient lore of the early twelfth century. He was an Englishman by birth, who studied in France, visited south Italy and Sicily and worked for some years in the Near East. Between 1114 and 1120 he discovered and translated an Arabic version of the *Elements*. Adelard is not known to have been personally interested in design; but he observed some of the architectural wonders of the Arab world, and thus forms a remarkable link between the educated western patron and one at least of the stylistic sources of the Gothic style.

On the whole, the technology of high vaults and the design of pointed arches must have been a matter for the architects and the skilled masons, the geometry of proportion and the choice of iconographic themes matter for the patrons. But it is clear that it was often not so simple as this. Once a tradition of ideas and themes was established, the architects themselves were quite capable of taking it in hand. Not for nothing was the phrase master mason (as the architects were called), master of the masons, whatever it originally meant, interpreted in the twelfth and thirteenth centuries to mean teacher, instructor of the masons. In a number of cases, however, it is clear that the influence of the patron went much further than this. It used to be thought, under the influence of the Romantic school of monastic history, that it was common, perhaps normal, for the monks to build their own monasteries. G. G. Coulton and his disciples made merry with this theory a generation ago; and it has been a common practice over the last fifty years to denigrate the monk-craftsman and minimize his importance. In some ways the reaction went too far; and it is clear that the story of monastic participation varies very much in different areas and in different arts and crafts. There is no doubt that all craftsmanship was characteristically the work of lay professionals after 1200. Even book production and the forgery of charters, traditional monastic arts, passed largely into the hands of secular professionals in the second half of the twelfth century.

THE PRESENTATION OF
CHURCHES BY THEIR
PATRONS

65, 66, 67 The idea portrayed in
these three examples is that a
new-built church is an offering
to God, the patron saint and
their earthly representative. Left,
from Avenas, King Louis –
possibly Louis VI of France
(1108–37) – presents the church
to St Vincent. Left below, the
sculptor Gilbert shows the
presentation of Autun cathedral,
probably by the duke of
Burgundy to the bishop of
Autun. Right, King William II
of Sicily (1166–89) offers
Monreale cathedral to the
Blessed Virgin

The notable products of late Anglo-Saxon painting in the tenth and eleventh centuries are generally presumed mainly the work of monks, and were directly inspired by St Dunstan and St Ethelwold, both of them competent and keen painters. In fine metalwork monks seem to have had something like a monopoly in England, inaugurated, once again, by the monastic reformers. This tradition was broken by the Norman Conquest, and there is no evidence of monastic dominance on this scale elsewhere. But the most striking evidence of monastic craftsmanship comes from Germany in the early twelfth century, in the shape of the treatise on *The Various Arts* by a German monk who wrote under the pseudonym Theophilus, and two elaborate portable altars and reliquaries in Paderborn made by Roger, monk of Helmarshausen, in 1100 and 1118. It is indeed highly probable that Roger and Theophilus were one and the same man. One of the special interests of Theophilus' treatise is that one can see the whole range of thought from the patron's mind and devout purposes through to the minute technical details of craftsmanship in a single book. It is an extraordinary link between the world of early medieval symbolism and twelfth century theology and the fashion of the Italian Renaissance for practical manuals – it is nearer in content to such works as Piero della Francesca on Perspective than to anything else of its own age, and it is no coincidence that the most divergent views have been held on its date and origin. Its most recent editor, Professor C. R. Dodwell, has set a provenance in Germany and the early twelfth century beyond reasonable doubt.

68 St Dunstan at Christ's feet; from a contemporary drawing ascribed to Dunstan himself

eidem eccle crucem auream quam ...
nostre que inpaderburne est st matri ecclesie transtulimus. necnon et scrinium quod nostro sumptu. frater eiusdem...
Rogerus satis expolito opere inhonorem sci kyliani atq: liborii fabricauerat. Crucis uero atq: scrinii. banni ac pisca...
ideo fecimus mentionem. ut nouerint succedentes nobis. deo traditum quod accepimus. nec destruendum quod s...
Vt igitur hec statuta perpetuo firma nobis ynostreq: illiq: ecclesie defunctis etiam prenotati permaneant. h...
bi tussimus et sigilli nostri inpressione signauimus. Ranno queq: domini nostri ihu xpi. et beatissimi apto...
xpi petri. nostraq: quam accepimus. ligandi atq: soluendi auctoritate. firmauimus et firmamus. Siquis aute...
ringere. uel destruere presumpserit. sese cum omnibus sibi cooprantib; anathemate perpetuo abeo quem offendit...
petro. dampnatum nouerit.

xviii Septembris. Anno dnice incarnat ostillo centes. indictione. viii. Ordinat uero hanrici epi. anno. x

ROGER, MONK OF HELMARSHAUSEN

69 An extract from a document, dated 1100, describing the portable altar, or
reliquary coffer ('scrinium') 'which brother Roger of the same church had
made with well-skilled craftsmanship in honour of Sts Kylianus and Liborius'

70 Roger's portable altar in Paderborn cathedral. This face shows five
Apostles – James, Philip, Paul, Bartholomew and Matthew

71 Chartres cathedral is one of the supreme surviving examples of how 'a building may be embellished with a variety of colours, without excluding the light of the day . . .' (p. 109)

Theophilus deals with the small-scale arts of his day in which monks engaged on a considerable scale: with book illumination, glass making, especially the art of stained glass windows, and, at far the greatest length, with metalwork, certainly his own speciality. The two latter were mainly for the adornment of churches; and the section on stained glass contains this account of his purpose:

God is mindful of the humble and quiet man, the man working in silence in the name of the Lord, obedient to the precept of Blessed Paul the Apostle: 'but rather let him labour, working with his hands the thing which is good that he may have to give to him that needeth.' Desiring to follow this man, I have approached the temple of holy wisdom, and beheld the sanctuary filled with a variety of all kinds of diverse colours with the usefulness and nature of each one set forth. Entering forthwith unobserved, I have filled the

Here Charlemagne presides over the building of the church of St James, Pamplona (the window is of *c.* 1210–20)

72 A monk cuts timber – though probably not for making glass, since he is a Cistercian (see p. 133)

storehouse of my heart with a sufficiency of all those things . . . and have clearly set them forth for your study, having examined them all individually with careful trial and proved them all with hand and eye. But since [glass-painting] cannot be translucent, I have, like a diligent seeker, taken particular pains to discover by what ingenious techniques a building may be embellished with a variety of colours, without excluding the light of the day and the rays of the sun. Having applied myself to this task, I understand the nature of glass, and I consider that this object can be obtained simply by the correct use of glass and its variety. This art, as I have learned from what I have seen and heard, I have endeavoured to unravel for your use.

Then we rapidly descend to earth. 'If you should decide to make glass, first cut plenty of beechwood logs and dry them . . .' and so forth.

Not unnaturally, Theophilus has most to say of the higher inspiration of the arts when he approaches his own craft of metalwork. In the preface to the third book he reminds his reader of how David (that is, the Psalmist) had said: 'Lord, I have loved the beauty of thy House'. But David did not merit to build the House of God,

73 Passage from Theophilus quoted on this page

'and entrusted almost all the needful resources in gold, silver, bronze and iron to his son Solomon. For he had read in *Exodus* that the Lord had given to Moses a commandment to build a tabernacle, and had chosen by name the masters of the work, and had filled them with the spirit of wisdom and understanding and knowledge in all learning for contriving and making works in gold and silver, bronze, gems, wood and in art of every kind. By pious reflection he had discerned that God delighted in embellishment of this kind, the execution of which He assigned to the power and guidance of the Holy Spirit, and he believed that nothing of this kind could be endeavoured without His inspiration.'

Thus Theophilus represents with admirable clarity the pious end of the spectrum in the motives for ornament and building in the twelfth century – a spectrum which included the love of display, of extravagance and social rivalry, which manifestly inspired some of the patrons and builders of the age.

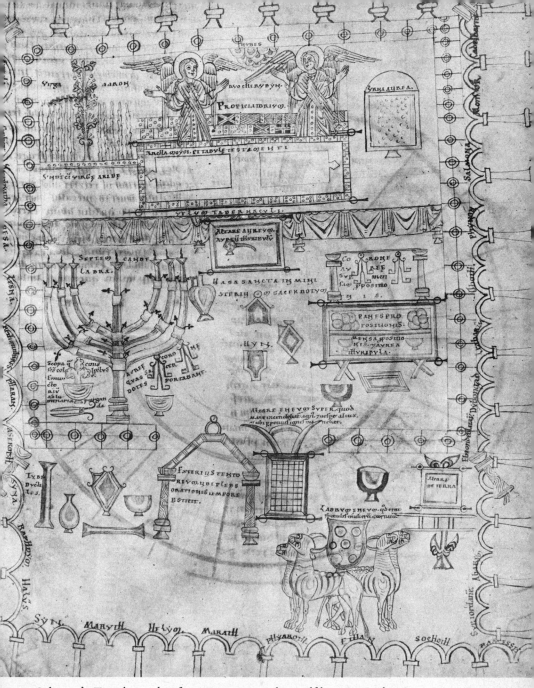

74 Solomon's Temple; a plan from Germany, early twelfth century, showing the temple and its ornaments, 'in gold and silver . . .'

75, 76 The joys of heaven and rewards of eternal life portrayed in the twelfth century mosaic of the Last Judgment on the west wall of Torcello cathedral. The details shown here are Heaven (above) and the Judgment and Hell (opposite)

'Wherefore, dearest son, when you have adorned His House with such embellishment and with such variety of work, you will not doubt, but believe with a full faith, that your heart has been filled with the Spirit of God.' And to quieten any doubts in the disciple, Theophilus lays out the ways in which the seven gifts of the Spirit direct and help the artist's work – from the spirit of wisdom and understanding which teach that all things created proceed from God and provide the necessary skill, the order, variety and measure with which one proceeds, to the spirit of godliness and fear of the Lord, by which one regulates the nature of the work – including the amount of the reward, 'lest the vice of avarice or cupidity steal in' – and teaches us in the end that we do nothing of ourselves but what is accorded by God.

Animated, dearest son, by these supporting virtues, you have approached the House of God with confidence, and have adorned it with so much beauty; you have embellished the ceilings or walls with varied work in different colours and have, in some measure, shown to beholders the paradise of God, glowing with varied flowers, verdant with herbs and foliage, and cherishing with crowns of varying merit the

'. . . THE VESSELS OF THE HOUSE OF GOD . . .'

77 Cover for a Gospel Book (*c.* 1000). The central panel of Christ, surrounded by foliage, was added in the twelfth century

78 A small German reliquary from Bamberg, made of a late classical onyx set with jewels

souls of the saints. You have given them cause to praise the Creator in the creature and proclaim Him wonderful in His works. For the human eye is not able to consider on what work first to fix its gaze; if it beholds the ceilings they glow like brocades; if it considers the walls they are a kind of paradise; if it regards the profusion of light from the windows, it marvels at the inestimable beauty of the glass and the infinitely rich and various workmanship. But if, perchance, the faithful soul observes the representation of the Lord's Passion expressed in art, it is stung with compassion. If it sees how many torments the saints endured in their bodies and what rewards of eternal life they have received, it eagerly embraces the observance of a better life. If it beholds how great are the joys of heaven and how great the torments in the infernal flames, it is animated by the hope of its good deeds and is shaken with fear by reflection on its sins.

And so the disciple is stirred to the utmost exertion of mind and skill to execute 'what is still lacking in the vessels of the house of God . . .: chalices, candlesticks, censers, cruets, shrines, reliquaries for holy relics, crosses, covers for Gospel Books and the rest. . . .'[23]

79 A twelfth century reliquary, also German – the Eltenberg Reliquary from Cologne

80 A bust-reliquary of Saint Baudime from Saint-Nectaire in France, end of the twelfth century

Theophilus gives us a vivid impression of a richly painted, glazed and ornamented Romanesque church of the early twelfth century. He shows plainly that at least in the decoration of a great church, a monk could himself take the leading part in design and craftsmanship; it may be that it was less common for a monk to be a master mason – we cannot tell. It was certainly possible. John, monk of Vendôme, was seconded as an expert mason to help in the building of Le Mans cathedral early in the twelfth century, and it is clear that he was so useful to Bishop Hildebert that he sheltered him from his abbot, who wrote letter after letter demanding his return. At one time Hildebert even provided John with an alibi, saying he had gone on pilgrimage to Jerusalem. We do not know the end of the story: the abbot disappears from view, fulminating anathemas at John the mason, 'a monk indeed, but one who lacks the masonry of charity'.

81 A chalice from Rheims of the twelfth century; from Toledo cathedral

82 Jesus as a boy, in royal robes; also from Toledo, thirteenth century (Spanish)

Of the vast majority of churches in this period, we have no precise idea how they were built, who the craftsmen and the architects were, beyond what can be deduced from the appearance of the result. But the documents sometimes, and the style of the completed work perhaps more often, give decisive evidence that style was not dictated by the patron.

The great church of St Lazarus at Autun is a powerful example of the failure of historical labels. It was begun in the 1120s, and was one of the last great French churches to be designed before the Gothic era opened with Suger's rebuilding of Saint-Denis near Paris. Its proportions are traditional – it shows none of the craving for height of the late twelfth century Gothic. It owes much, including the greatest of its craftsmen, to the supreme works of eastern French Romanesque of the previous generation, the abbeys of Cluny and Vézelay. It is therefore reckoned to be the culmination of Romanesque, not the *fons et origo* of Gothic.[24] From this we might suppose that it was a fine building, but notably unoriginal. It is indeed the case that its pointed arches, and the fluting on the face of the arcade, were almost certainly imitated from the third church at Cluny; and that the abbot or architect of Cluny had himself probably seen pointed arches in another great building of the age no longer extant, the abbey of Monte Cassino, which was perhaps in this respect based directly on Moslem architecture. Yet St Lazarus, Autun, as well as showing the influence of Islam, also reveals classical influence to a degree quite unusual for the twelfth century, both in a part of its architectural design and in the technique of its sculpture. There is indeed some point in the emphasis of the experts that this is a Romanesque building; it had great influence on the future, but its influence is not to be compared with that of Saint-Denis. Yet in a sense it reveals the bankruptcy of labels. It has elements of Romanesque, it has some elements of Gothic; but it is essentially a building of the renaissance.

The main architectural theme is a remarkable combination of the elevation of Cluny III[25] and a Roman arch still extant in the city, whose influence is particularly evident in the triforium. The effect is impressive, and gives a strong sense of design and direction; yet there is a marked contrast between the broad architectural effect and the sculpted capitals by Gislebertus, Gilbert, one of the greatest of Romanesque sculptors. One conspicuous feature of Gilbert's art was the use of chisels and drills to produce sharp contrasts of light and shade, a technique reminiscent of late Roman sculpture. The tools had been known and used in the early Middle Ages; but this particular technique, which makes Gilbert's figures exceptionally rounded and alert, was novel in the early twelfth century. It seems clear that, once embarked on their projects, the bishop or the canons of Autun became aware of what was afoot at Cluny and Vézelay, and employed craftsmen who had learned or per-

83, 84 The few fragments of sculpture surviving from Cluny have much to tell us of Gilbert's early career. Some are by Gilbert himself; others, like the Fourth Tone of Music, right, provided models for his work on the same themes at Autun. Far right, the Fourth Tone at Autun

fected their trades in those great churches. Beyond that point it seems likely that they left the design to their craftsmen, since it seems improbable that they deliberately conceived an artistic plan based on two inspirations, whose divergence is evidently more conspicuous at Autun than it ever was at Cluny.

In this case we may be tolerably sure that the dominant note in the style of the church as we see it was not dictated by the patrons, but they certainly seem to have appreciated the result. The culmination of Gilbert's work was the magnificent Last Judgment on the tympanum over the west door. Here, beneath Christ's feet, amid inscriptions full of the thunder of judgment, are the words 'Gislebertus hoc fecit': 'This is Gilbert's work.' It is the only record we have of Gilbert save what may be deduced from this work, but it is a notable record. There was nothing unusual in this age for the craftsmen's name to be recorded; but this inscription is quite exceptionally conspicuous,

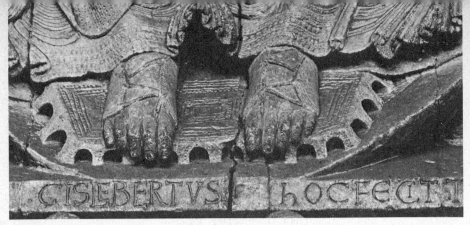

GISLEBERTVS HOCFECIT

85, 86 'Gislebertus hoc fecit' – 'This is Gilbert's work': above, the sculptor's signature at Christ's feet in the Last Judgment over the west door at Autun. Below, an angel and a devil, characteristically elongated, weigh souls in the Last Judgment

and one may assume that its placing reflects both the dedication of the work at Christ's feet implicit in Theophilus' prefaces and some self-portraits of scribes in illuminated manuscripts, and also the pride of creation. The iconographical scheme was no doubt dictated by the patron, but the style and the detailed planning as well as the execution were Gilbert's; and the sculpture of Autun is quite unusual in its own age in being in a large measure the personal creation of a named artist. In their brilliant reconstruction of his work, the Abbé Grivot and Professor Zarnecki conclude: 'He was, in fact, the only [Romanesque] artist whose work survives' from France in this

87 Gilbert's *Eve* (see p. 123)

88 This Gallo-Roman relief from the Beaune Museum illustrates the classical inspiration of Gilbert's *Eve*, as was pointed out in D. Grivot and G. Zarnecki, *Gislebertus*, p. 149

period, 'who carried out a lavish sculptural decoration of a large church practically alone during at least ten years of continual work'.[26] In all these respects he reminds us of the world of the Italian Renaissance.

The classical influence appears most clearly in Gilbert's *Eve*, in which the relation between feminine beauty and original sin (in itself a theme of the age without much warrant in the book of Genesis) is portrayed with a combination of delicacy and sensuous frankness with no parallel in Romanesque art; but the imagery has close links with classical sculpture and the sentiment with some of the vernacular literature of the late twelfth and early thirteenth centuries. In other respects Gilbert's treatment of drama, human and divine, is more characteristic of his age: a part of his technique lay in the use of fluttering draperies, especially familiar in pre-Conquest English drawings and in the French books which they inspired, though also to be found elsewhere on the Continent. Another of Gilbert's traits is the elongation of the human body – an instance of the way he and his contemporaries normally repudiated static nature for the sake of feeling and drama – which in its turn inspired the greatest figure sculptures of the next age at Chartres.

CRAFTSMEN AND THEIR SIGNATURES

89 Left above, Girauldus, sculptor of the twelfth century tympanum at Saint-Ursin, Bourges

90 Far left, 'W. de Brail' me fecit'. The painter is rescued in the Last Judgment; from a manuscript of *c.* 1240

91 Left, Hugo Pictor: the Anglo-Norman painter Hugh in a manuscript of *c.* 1100

92 Right, the sculptor on the bronze doors of S. Zeno Maggiore, Verona; twelfth century (German)

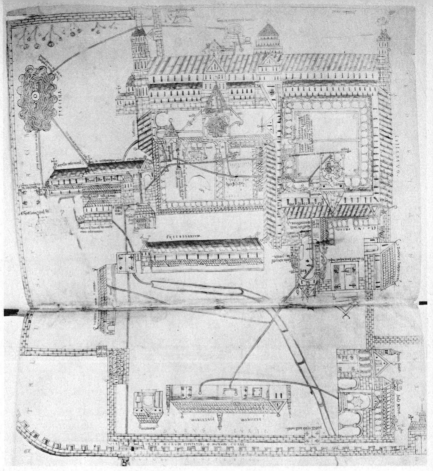

93 Canterbury cathedral priory. Plan of the precinct and its waterworks from the Eadwine Psalter, the only surviving monastic plan of its kind from the twelfth century. It shows that the Cistercians did not have a monopoly of advanced plumbing in this age (see p. 139)

CANTERBURY AND WILLIAM OF SENS

The bishop and canons of Autun put themselves in Gilbert's hands in the 1120s; Abbot Suger took his most fateful decisions in the 1130s and 1140s. Over the next generation the crucial designs were made which created the Gothic of the Île de France. Some of the human elements in this are summed up in the story of the best documented Gothic cathedral of the late twelfth century. Four years after the murder of Thomas Becket in 1170 the choir of Canterbury cathedral was conveniently gutted by fire, and the monks given the opportunity of re-building it as a monument to the martyr. The account in Gervase's chronicle of what happened is fascinating from a variety of viewpoints. He does not give the impression that the monks were immediately impressed with the opportunity given them – no doubt many were daunted by the cost and upheaval of a major work. They interviewed a whole series of masons – the scene in Dorothy Sayers' *Zeal of thy House* gives a fair impression of this – and finally chose William of Sens, clearly one of the most forceful and ambitious of those they consulted. The choir of Canterbury cathedral is very fine, but it is an eccentricity among English buildings of the age, without native precursors and with few native successors. It is obviously a representative of the proto-Gothic of the Île de France, and even if Gervase had never written, the work at Sens cathedral begun in the 1140s would have been noted as one probable source of inspiration; though one only, for the Canterbury choir is an anthology of motifs from contemporary work in northern France.[27] Sens had been one of Becket's homes, and a number of his old associates (though none of the monks) were very familiar with it; the link might also have suggested to William of Sens that Canterbury was a place to try his hand. There is, however, no suggestion of this sort of background in Gervase's account, which describes the medieval equivalent of an architects' competition; and by the 1170s William had evidently travelled widely, as his design reveals. Sens is the earliest cathedral, in Mr Harvey's words, 'universally regarded as Gothic'.[28] 'The germs of Gothic' may clearly be seen at Saint-Denis; in Sens they are fully present; the design of the choir of Canterbury descends from Sens and several other buildings of its type and age. When the scaffolding gave way in 1178 and William fell fifty feet to the pavement and had (not unnaturally) to take to his bed, the work was carried on under the direction of a young monk. The monk took instruc-tions from the bedridden architect, and supervised the work

125

himself. This was clearly intended as an interim measure: a twelfth century master mason could not give the close supervision that was needed from a sickbed. Despairing of full recovery, William of Sens returned home, and William the Englishman ruled in his stead; but he completed the task on the lines already laid down by his eminent namesake.

At Autun and Canterbury the initiative in style and design seems mainly to have come from the professional master masons, not from the patrons. One would assume that this was already the normal situation, and perhaps had long been so. But Autun and Canterbury are quite exceptional buildings, and in many cases a very substantial element of choice is likely

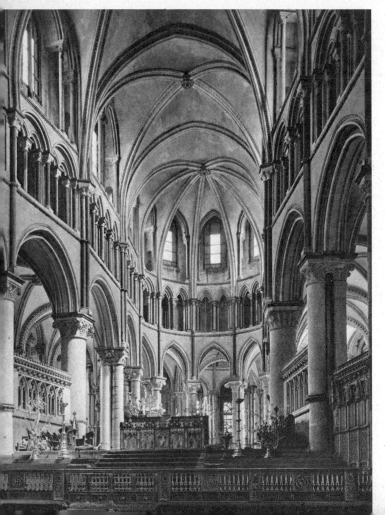

94 Canterbury cathedral choir. The shape and proportions of the bay reveal the influence of Sens cathedral; other elements in the design show that William of Sens had travelled widely among the Gothic churches of northern France

to have lain with the patron. The design of a great church was based on contemporary conceptions of its function, and on fashion: on function the patrons must always have given the lead, and in those cases where fashion was slavishly followed, they may have had the sort of freedom of choice enjoyed by the patrons of French châteaux and Scottish baronial castles in the late nineteenth century. One would tend to think that the master masons showed their freedom and inventiveness most clearly in original buildings like Autun or Canterbury and the other great Gothic churches, and that their architects were forerunners of the notable thirteenth century architects, some of whom are more than mere names to us.

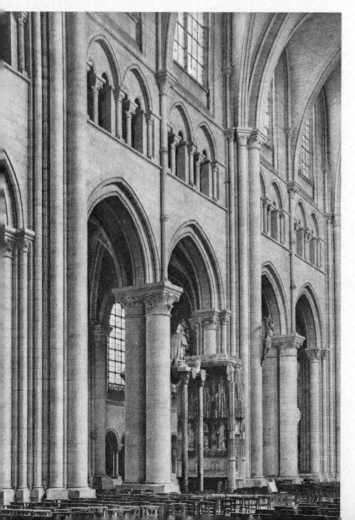

95 Sens cathedral, one of the earliest French Gothic cathedrals, begun in the 1140s

127

To this there is one notable and famous exception. The influence of Abbot Suger in the abbey of Saint-Denis, the cradle of Gothic, went very much further. Suger was a monk, an administrator, a royal minister, a notable author, and a great patron of artists and architects. The combination is at once unique and characteristic of the age. He himself tells us how one rainy day the workmen at the quarry near Pontoise reckoned it was impossible to continue hauling the stone up and loading the wagons needed for the building work at Saint-Denis; and how the saint himself came to the aid of a heroic group of boys and cripples, who were able to haul up blocks from the bottom of a chasm which would normally have taxed the strength of 140 – or at any rate 100 – men. Suger's own writings on the rebuilding of his abbey are a quarry as miraculous as the quarry near Pontoise, and have been as extensively worked. He was not without his vanity. He tells us much of his own work for the building, but never mentions the name of any of his craftsmen. Perhaps he thought that his audience, like his fellow-Parisian, the theologian Hugh of Saint-Victor, reckoned architecture a base, mechanical art. Although something is clearly hidden from us, it would be excessively sceptical to doubt that Suger gives a fair and accurate picture of his own influence; and although its precise limits cannot be set, its general lines are clear enough. Suger had an extraordinarily wide range of interests. A great deal of space is taken up with the logistics of the operation: the way he increased the productivity of a part of the estates and set it aside as basic revenue – the remaining three-quarters of the funds coming from offerings at the shrine of St Denis and other gifts. At the other extreme, he shows the symbolic idea underlying the scheme: most notably how he, like Theophilus, was fascinated by light. Suger was quite self-conscious in his aim to make Saint-Denis a church in which the light shineth in darkness and the darkness comprehendeth it not; and it is clear that the light reflected in precious stones had a particular attraction to him. He says specifically that the mind is drawn to God by contemplation of these sparkling lights; and it seemed peculiarly appropriate to experiment with the play of light in jewelled reliquaries and stained glass windows in a church dedicated to the saint most closely associated with the symbolism of light. One can imagine the indignation of the monks of Saint-Denis when their fellow monk Peter Abelard, exercising a little historical criticism, threw doubt on the identification of the symbolical writer now commonly known as the Pseudo-Dionisius with their own patron.

Suger was moved to rebuild by the dangerous state of some of the fabric, and the plain fact that the building was too small: he delighted to describe the fearful crush of pilgrims on the great festivals of the saint, so that the monks deputed to show the relics had to leap out of a window to avoid being crushed to death. He provided for a much enlarged choir and ambulatory to be the setting for a new and richly adorned shrine, and a much enlarged west end. But the main nave arcade of the Carolingian church was left for the time being.

'In carrying out such plans my first thought was for the concordance and harmony of the ancient and the new work. By reflection, by inquiry, and by investigation through different regions of remote districts, we endeavoured to learn where we might obtain marble columns or columns the equivalent thereof. Since we found none, only one thing was left to us, distressed in mind and spirit: we might obtain them', says the abbot in a vein of unaccustomed fantasy, 'from Rome (for in Rome we had often seen wonderful ones in the Palace of Diocletian and other Baths) by safe ships through the Mediter-ranean, thence through the English sea and the tortuous windings of the River Seine, at great expense to our friends and even under convoy of our enemies, the near-by Saracens. For many years, for a long time, we were perplexed, thinking and making enquiries – when suddenly the generous munifi-cence of the Almighty, condescending to our labours, revealed

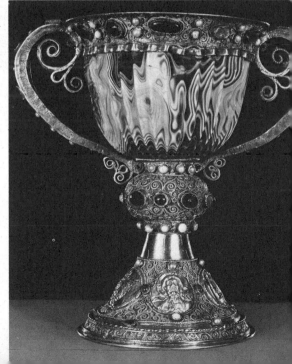

96 Suger himself, as donor, in a
window at Saint-Denis

97 Far left, an antique vase of
Egyptian porphyry, characteristically adapted for use in Saint-Denis
by Suger

98 Left, one of Suger's chalices,
partly Greco-Roman. The brilliant
jewels, in his view, are a reflection
of God's glory and so attract the
beholder's eye to meditation

99 Right, a group of Suger's columns
on the west door of Saint-Denis

to the astonishment of all and through the merit of the Holy Martyrs, what one would never have thought or imagined: very fine and excellent [columns] . . .' And he goes on to describe the discovery that the old quarry near Pontoise, hitherto a source of nothing more elegant than millstones, had suitable stone of high quality deep in its chasm – just what was needed for the work.[29]

Besides stone, a great building needed a massive supply of timber, temporarily for scaffolding, permanently for the structure of the roof above the vault. He tells us how he lay awake one night after mattins (the midnight office), worrying about where to find large timbers; then had an inspiration, leapt out of bed and led an expedition into one of his forests. Both these stories show Suger's direct interest in choice of style and materials; and over the whole of his writings on Saint-Denis broods the person of the saint, whose relics and shrine were the centre and inspiration of the whole work, who personally presided over his abbey and provided the means for its rebuilding.

100 The base of a cross. Suger's great cross is lost, but this base, from Saint-Bertin (Saint-Omer) was an imitation of it

The excellent Theophilus insisted on the value of work. In this the founders of the Cistercian Order agreed with him, though in little else. It is true that among the early monks were some expert illuminators (including perhaps Abbot Stephen Harding himself); but this was firmly forbidden after a while, and under the inspiration of St Bernard a total repudiation of visual ornament or art of every kind was enforced. This represented a doctrine the exact opposite of Suger's. Suger argued that the sparkling light of jewels carried the mind to God; Bernard that the ornament and the proportions of the great churches of his day – most notably of Cluny – distracted the mind. Precious metal, ornament, paint, coloured glass, sculpture, were all forbidden. If one examines Cistercian remains closely it becomes clear that this ruthless exclusion of so much that most men of the age delighted in was beyond the bounds even of Cistercian human nature in its prime. The spirit if not the letter of this doctrine was broken here and there. And certain alleviations came in as soon as Bernard was safely dead. The rigorous logic behind the Cistercian style suggests that Bernard had a considerable personal share in its devising. But the main points survived long after his death: the general chapter could warn a potential benefactor at the end of the century that the old monastery he was offering to give the Order must be rebuilt according to the Cistercian customs; and more than one Cistercian abbot had the experience of seeing his new building scheme demolished under the stern direction of the visitor. A change took place after the end of the century. Up till then the plan and style of Cistercian abbeys were extraordinarily uniform all over Europe. Local variations, local expressions of style, adaptations to geographical conditions there were, but when all allowances have been made, the uniformity of plan and the uniformity of style make Cistercian architecture one of the striking phenomena of the twelfth century; a great historical document from

133

whatever point we view it. To a remarkable degree Cistercian monasteries were complete by 1200 or soon after, and it is striking how high a proportion of surviving Cistercian buildings comes from the twelfth century. But they sometimes rebuilt, especially in countries where monasticism and the Baroque flourished together; and the churches which are later, even those like Rievaulx or Tintern which are of the thirteenth century, are normal representatives of their age. This underlines the astonishing achievement in preserving uniformity in early days.

'They have built their monasteries with their own labour in deserted or woodland places', wrote the Benedictine monk Orderic Vitalis in 1133–34, 'and with adroit forethought they have laid on them sacred names, such as Domus Dei, Claravallis [Clairvaux], Bonus Mons, Eleemosyna [L'Aumône] and many others of this kind; and those who hear these names are allured solely by the nectar of a name in haste to find out how great is the blessedness denoted by such a special title.' Walter Map the satirist later (c. 1181) added the rider that 'desert places they do assuredly either find or make'.[30] Be that as it may, Orderic is an early witness to the tradition that the Cistercians built their own monasteries. A year or so after he wrote, there occurred a crisis in the affairs of Bernard's own Clairvaux; the abbey had to be moved to a more ample site. Bernard's biographer tells us that when the saint had been brought down to earth and had said his prayers and made some characteristically shrewd practical dispositions, the great men of the neighbourhood provided funds and resources.

101 The handwriting of Orderic Vitalis – the end of
Book VI of his *Historia Ecclesiastica* 'EXPLICIT LIBER SEXTUS . . .', written in 1141

Supplies were abundant, workmen quickly hired, the brothers themselves joined in the work in every way: some cut timbers, others shaped stones, others built walls, others divided the river, set it in new channels and lifted the leaping waters to the mill-wheels; fullers and bakers and tanners and smiths and other artificers prepared suitable machines for their tasks, that the river might flow fast and do good wherever it was needed in every building, flowing freely in underground conduits; the streams performed suitable tasks in every office and cleansed the abbey and at length returned to the main course and restored to the river what it had lost. The walls which gave the abbey a spacious enclosure were finished with unlooked-for speed. The abbey rose; the new-born church, as if it had a living soul that moveth, quickly developed and grew.[31]

It was natural that the Cistercians, who attracted a wide variety of men of initiative and talent in their early days, should find, especially among the lay brothers, a certain number of skilled masons; and they probably benefited from the fact that the building industry must have been exceptionally large in early twelfth century Europe, lying at the end of a century and a half of what would nowadays be called a building explosion. It was also natural that their supply of recruits from men of special talent should grow thinner in the thirteenth century, as the inspiration passed to other Orders, and this may partly account for the disappearance of the Cistercian style. It is, however, most unlikely that all Cistercian abbeys were built by Cistercian monks. Bernard's *Life* clearly indicates that the monks were assisted by lay professionals. There is a little direct evidence here and there that there were lay master masons, and also that hired craftsmen were a fairly normal part of the scene. Among the monks of Clairvaux directly associated with this sort of work were the novice-master Achard, 'founder and devoted builder of very many abbeys', and Geoffrey d'Ainai, who among other activities

came to England to start the stone buildings of Fountains abbey and instruct the monks from St Mary's York in the Cistercian code. But these men were not specialist builders, and it is difficult to know to what extent they were master masons. The cases in which this is clear all refer to lay brothers. No doubt Geoffrey d'Ainai was well informed on the Cistercian style and plan, and we may be reasonably certain that he took a master mason with him, or had some means of transmitting from craftsmen to craftsmen the essential information. We may be tolerably sure that among the anonymous lay brothers who were masons lay the technical knowledge and skill which made the Cistercian achievement possible. It also seems likely that it was in St Bernard's Clairvaux, rather than in the Order's

102 Fountains abbey. The west
front of the church and the lay
brothers' quarters: an impressive
monument of Cistercian
simplicity and of the scale of a
large Cistercian house

103 Fontenay abbey, looking
east. The light shines through
plain glass into a bare church –
originally furnished, but simply;
never painted or adorned

mother house at Cîteaux, that the Cistercian plan was perfected.
One of its striking features was the shallow, square-ended
presbytery, designed to be a marked contrast to the traditional
semi-circular apse. Some very early Cistercian churches were
rectangular boxes; some had single apses; but this shallow,
square presbytery seems essentially to be a feature of the second
stage in Cistercian building, from *c.* 1125 to St Bernard's
death in 1153. In this period it was almost invariably used. No
sooner was Bernard gone than there was an outbreak of apses,
even in Clairvaux itself, where his sanctuary was rebuilt in the
years immediately following his death. None the less, the
square, shallow presbytery remained the commonest in the
Cistercian repertoire until the end of the century.[32]

Even more characteristic of the relation of the Cistercians to the intellectual movements of their age was the system of proportions they devised in planning their churches. The Cistercians, and in particular St Bernard, were puritanical, even in some respects philistine. Bernard repudiated all ornament and refused to be bound by the rules of Latin metre; he is notorious for his attacks on the theological adventures of Abelard and Gilbert de la Porrée. Yet he was also the author of some of the most ornamental prose of the century: in this single medium no effort, no rhetorical art should be spared in God's service. In two particular respects he and his Order were particularly involved in the intellectual world of their day.

The basis of their life was the *Rule* of St Benedict, read as if it had never been read before: they took it off the shelf, as Irnerius took the *Digest*, blew away the cobwebs and the glosses of centuries, and read it with fresh eyes – no simple task, but the work of sophisticated and educated minds. And Bernard himself, and a few others of his kind – most notably the English St Ailred of Rievaulx – shared to the full the interest in human emotion and its expression which is one aspect of twelfth century humanism. In this, unintentionally and half-unconsciously, Bernard and Abelard were at one, though the difference remained profound, since in Bernard's thought the love of man for man counted only as a shadow of the love of God for man, and its expression could only be justified by its subservience to the love of God. Yet however this may be, the sense of human love in his famous lament for his brother, or the sense of human contact which we can still feel after eight centuries in the best of his letters, makes Bernard's the most effective witness of human self-expression of his age.

This helps us to understand that the ruthless puritanism of Cistercian design was no accidental philistinism, but a sophisticated, reflected, studied attitude, with the inspiration of Bernard behind it. The aim was to avoid all distraction; to help the mind to concentrate; and working to this brief the Cistercian master builders devised a model which gave plenty of space for monks and lay brothers, was dignified and serviceable, but carefully avoided the excessive height and inordinate breadth (in Bernard's own words) of the great church at Cluny, and all the fascinating wealth of sculpture, including the works of the young Gilbert, and paint and glass; a whitewashed, open barn using the latest devices, mathematical proportion and the pointed arch, for the opposite purpose to that intended elsewhere – to avoid catching the eye or disturbing the concentration of the mind.

The quality of Cistercian building was generally high, the masonry fine; the Cistercians showed a special interest in the design of conduits and drains, which made them pioneers in plumbing, just as they were pioneers in the use of watermills for various occupations more complicated than grinding corn. All this presupposes a group of highly proficient masons within the Order, and indicates the peculiar success of the Cistercians in recruiting men of many crafts. There is a notable difference between their standards and those of the early Norman buildings in England, where it is clear that an ambitious building programme outran the country's resources in skilled masons for a generation or so. It is unlikely that the Cistercians could have maintained their standards without a great deal of local, expert help. But they seem normally to have lent a hand in building themselves, and in some, perhaps many cases, they provided the nucleus of the skilled labour force. This has sometimes led to their being described as amateur builders, but there was certainly nothing amateurish about them. In their work patron and builder came closer together than in any other type of building known to us; the old tradition of monastic craftsmanship (under somewhat strange circumstances) enjoyed its Indian summer, deliberately fostered by the Order's insistence that manual labour was an essential part of the monastic life, by its very substantial recruitment of lay brothers, and by its constant wish to be self-sufficient, isolated from the world.

The shallow, rectangular presbytery is in some ways the most striking of the Cistercians' innovations. In this, as in the use of the pointed arch, they were pioneers of changes which were to have a great future. The altar in earlier centuries had been the centre of the church, with the bishop's throne or the equivalent behind it, with no object upon it to hide the worshippers from the view of the bishop when he blessed them, though it was commonly surmounted by a canopy or ciborium. This arrangement is clearly intended in the picture of the bishop blessing in the *Benedictional of St Ethelwold*, a picture made intelligible by comparison with the arrangements described in some cathedrals such as Canterbury in the early twelfth century or with those we can still see in the choir of the same period at San Clemente in Rome. San Clemente would perhaps have appeared a little old-fashioned to Suger. In particular the ciborium stood in the way of a large raised shrine completing the vista behind the altar, such as Suger, or William of Sens, affected – not an entirely new fashion, since its origin goes back at least to the eighth century, but one which came to flourish only in this age. Suger was very advanced in having two candlesticks on his altar: one was the norm, accepted by the Cistercians, set at one side, with the Cross at the other to balance it, so that the view across the altar was still not obscured. From the thirteenth century on, the practice of having six candles on the altar during mass appeared and grew; but only at first for papal High Mass in the Roman basilicas, for only during the Counter-Reformation did a long row of candlesticks become part of the regular furnishing of altars anywhere in Christendom, only in the nineteenth did the practice penetrate to every corner of Catholic Christendom. But already by the end of the twelfth century, and perhaps in many places much earlier, it was no longer necessary to see anything to the east beyond the altar, except in some churches a very conspicuous shrine; for the celebrant was definitely established to the west of the altar, the bishop to the south. In order that the people might see the Body and Blood of Christ present in the sacrament, the practice of elevating the host and chalice had to be devised. The next step was to make the altar the end of the picture and hide even the shrine behind it with a reredos; and finally, in the fourteenth and fifteenth centuries, enormous screens of wood and stone broke up the long vista of late Romanesque and early Gothic churches into a series of boxes, proof against draughts and laymen.[33]

The Cistercians had no shrines or costly crucifixes, and they were therefore able to arrive at the idea of placing the altar, quite simply, against the east wall, in one jump. The apses built after St Bernard's death (however functional some might appear to be) seem to testify to a certain uneasiness among his colleagues about this revolutionary change. Yet in the long run the square end had a great success. It had been used in small churches in many parts before; the Cistercians could find precedents particularly in their own home country, in north-eastern France. In England it had been foreshadowed also in larger churches even before the Cistercian settlement: the shallow apses in a square frame, for instance, in Old Sarum cathedral could well have set an imaginative observer considering the effect of a square east end without the apses. This may be part of the reason why the future, in English Gothic churches, lay with the square end, while in French Gothic, and elsewhere, the apse survived. But we cannot doubt that the new English idiom, however far removed from St Bernard in spirit, was in part inspired by the proliferation of great Cistercian churches in the mid and late twelfth century. The great square-ended church was a natural setting for a long altar, adorned with many candles, and with a reredos behind it: these elements could live in a harmony always difficult to achieve in an apse. In the twentieth century, now that the celebrant commonly faces the people once again, the characteristic layout of the Gothic or Baroque altar is becoming an embarrassment; the wheel has come full cycle.

THE ALTAR

104 St Ethelwold blessing, with bare altar and low screens

105 Below, San Clemente, Rome, built in the early twelfth century, but preserving the traditional Roman arrangement. Almost everything except the candles on the altar is twelfth century or older

106 Right, two candles on the altar: *c.* 1085 (Bohemian)

107 Far right, two candles on and five behind the altar: twelfth century (Cluny)

108 Right below, the Gloucester candlestick: detail showing a man, strange beasts and two birds, part of a very complex design

The Cistercian story illustrates in a piquant way the mingling of local and universal elements in twelfth century fashion and art. The hints of Gothic on the one hand and the uniformity of style over many lands on the other represent the cosmopolitan nature of twelfth century culture. The Burgundian element in this style illustrates the local varieties, the special contribution of the various parts of Christendom – and the use of the pointed arch involved Islam too. Even more striking is the effect of studying some of the finer English illuminated manuscripts of the age, and considering the sources of their style. In the eleventh century England had been the home of one of the most flourishing schools of book illumination of the day. Some of its elements – its skill in draftsmanship, its love of drama, its fluttering draperies – came to influence the Continent at the end of the century (see p. 123). Some of its dramatic themes were too eccentric to be followed: the famous Weingarten Crucifixion of the mid-eleventh century portrayed the human Jesus on the Cross with a poignancy which can scarcely be paralleled till the fifteenth century. The cult of the human Jesus was indeed characteristic of the twelfth century, and this affected its art: but even in England the dominant mode in the twelfth century came to be the hieratic religious art of Byzantine paintings and mosaics. Long before western knights conquered Byzantium in the Crusade of 1204, Byzantium had established its empire in the west.

THE ST ALBANS PSALTER, HENRY OF BLOIS AND BYZANTINE INFLUENCES

In the second decade of the twelfth century (or *c.* 1120) scribes and artists in St Albans Abbey were preparing for their abbot's protégée Christina, the anchoress and prioress of Markyate, a book in which the cultural and religious sentiment of the age

109 The St Albans Psalter: The Visitation. This is an example of the attempt
to combine solidity in the figures with movement and even drama, which is
characteristic of the Psalter

is marvellously summarized. The St Albans Psalter contains rich materials, literary and visual, for the devotional life of a pious lady. Christina had been married as a young girl; but she had succeeded in convincing her husband that her real wish was to be an anchoress, not a wife, and her marriage was in due time annulled; and after a series of romantic adventures she ended happily as a respected nun and spiritual mother. Thus it was fitting that her Psalter should contain a somewhat romantic life, in Anglo-Norman (Norman French), of St Alexis, whose legend told a tale similar to hers. It also contained calendar, psalter, canticles, creed and Litany; a letter of Pope Gregory the Great supporting the use of craftsmanship for the instruction of the unlearned; over 200 painted initials; and, above all, over forty full-page paintings telling the Biblical story from Man's Fall to the Day of Pentecost. Some of the paintings show a precise and sophisticated elaboration of the spiritual or allegorical interpretation of the Bible – interpretations not in themselves new, though it is characteristic of the age that they should be so closely integrated in its art. Some of the initials to the Psalter reveal the literal interpretation also characteristic of contemporary Biblical scholarship; for in the twelfth century the literal as well as the allegorical and other modes of interpreting Scripture flourished and grew. But the fame of the book rests on the large Biblical scenes: for here one finds a new style of painting, of an originality which is striking evidence of an urge to new experiment, partly characteristic of the age, much more, one is bound to think, of the anonymous craftsmen who designed and executed it. Yet no single element in its art is wholly new. Its chief designer had absorbed something of all the major traditions of European painting of his day; and so one finds, powerfully if sometimes grotesquely united, the rich colours, and especially the greens and purples, of German painting of the tenth and eleventh centuries; the hieratic setting and solidity of Byzantine art; the concern with outline of Anglo-Saxon art; the dramatic intensity which Romanesque art at large attempted to substitute for any close approach to the naturalistic reproduction of human features. In its derivatives and successors, such as Henry of Blois' Psalter (see below) and the Winchester Bible, all these elements are still clearly present, and the former shows how the Byzantine influence continued to flow directly into England. But the sense of movement, the vivacity of Anglo-Saxon drawing meanwhile was reasserting itself. The St Albans Psalter has a quality of grandeur in marked contrast to the immediacy of the best of Anglo-Saxon. It is perhaps not entirely fanciful to find an analogy in the contrast between pontifical High Mass in the intimacy of the pre-Conquest cathedral of East Anglia at North Elmham, whose full extent barely exceeded 40 yards, and in Norwich cathedral, which was fully 150 yards long. A more penetrating insight is offered by Professor Wormald's suggestion that 'the contrast [between the Weingarten Crucifixion and the St Albans Psalter] bears something of that which exists between the short prayer that pierces unto Heaven and the grandeur and pageantry of a High Mass.'[34]

It is no chance that Byzantine influence flowed to England. Indeed, it had flowed there before, in pre-Conquest times; but in the twelfth century the two Norman kingdoms of England and Sicily had close cultural as well as political links, and the great churches of Sicily formed an entrepot between

110 Eastern influence. This twelfth century portable reliquary may be an Arab coffer made in Sicily or an English imitation. It is believed to have been used to fetch back St Petroc's bones when they had been stolen from Bodmin Priory (Cornwall) in 1177. It is now in St Petroc's parish church in Bodmin

Byzantium and England. Under the patronage of Roger the Great and his successors, Byzantine craftsmen constructed or inspired the construction of the mosaics at Cefalù and Monreale and in the Palatine chapel in Palermo. These are among the finest works of Byzantine art of the century, and the presence of Byzantine artists in Sicily illustrates very clearly one aspect of the theme of this chapter. Roger did not have to turn to the east for experts in mosaics. In his own time in Rome a school of native craftsmen were engaged in the local revival whose most remarkable fruit are the charming mosaics of San Clemente. Here patterns and themes drawn from the older basilica and half-understood classical motifs – including a platoon of Cupids – mingle in a field of green and gold as fresh today as when first constructed. Anglo-Norman diplomats, craftsmen and men of letters visited Rome often, Sicily from time to time; but it was Sicily which inspired the new ideas in English painting, and beyond Sicily, Byzantium.

There is a famous story told by John of Salisbury of how the prince-bishop of Winchester, Henry of Blois, King Stephen's brother, visited Rome in 1149–50, and, failing in the object of his mission, consoled himself by buying old statues and transporting them back to Winchester. None of these statues survive.[35] They were a rich collection made by one of the great patrons of the century, and a patron of cosmopolitan taste. His uncle, King Henry I, had lavished his wealth on Cluny when the younger Henry was a monk there; and Henry of Blois had no inhibitions in spending his own great wealth to foster craftsmanship and adorn his many churches. An inventory survives of his gifts to the cathedral – gospel books, crosses, frontals, carpets, embroidered tapestries, reliquaries and so forth; and a proportion of his gifts, or of works made under his patronage, still survives. Parts of his castles, especially his principal seat in Wolvesey Palace, the tower of his cathedral, the Church of St Cross outside Winchester testify to his architectural patronage. The font of Tournai marble, curiously rather than finely carved; copper plaques enamelled with a picture of the bishop carrying a reliquary, also probably from northern France or the Low Countries; and two magnificent books – such are the remains of a collection which once represented not only English, French, Flemish and Roman taste, but also German vestments and a Moslem carpet.

Nowhere in all this is there any clear indication that the bishop himself had visited Sicily or been inspired by Byzantium; yet the two books, the St Swithun's Psalter undoubtedly made at Winchester in his time, and the Winchester Bible probably representing the work of men brought up under his aegis, are eloquent testimony that Byzantine Sicily had inspired his craftsmen. Two pages in the Psalter, representing the death of the Virgin and her glorification, are so closely copied from Byzantine originals that they have been sometimes supposed the work of Byzantine artists. It is perhaps more likely, as Professor Zarnecki has suggested, that they were inspired by Byzantine artefacts – ivories, fabrics or the like – brought by Archbishop William of York, Henry's nephew who spent a period in exile in Italy and visited Sicily.[36] Of two of the original masters of the Winchester Bible, as Professor Otto Demus has said in his great book on *The Mosaics of Norman Sicily*, they 'must have been in Sicily and have actually studied the mosaics of Monreale. The attitudes, the draperies and, even more, the facial types of the figures illuminated by these Masters are more than echoes of the Monreale mosaics. Even the expression, the spiritual *habitus* of the faces, is very much the same.'[37] Nor was the influence of Monreale confined to books. One of the most impressive examples of English wall painting of the twelfth century, the bending figure of St Paul shaking the viper off his hand in the chapel of St Anselm at Canterbury, though in many respects reminiscent of the Bury Bible and so firmly planted in Anglo-Norman Romanesque traditions, is also strikingly similar to the figure of Paul in the Palatine chapel at Palermo, so that Demus has said that it is 'likely that the Canterbury painter knew the Palermitan mosaic'.[38]

111 Above, enamelled plaque commemorating Henry; now in the British Museum, probably from a reliquary given to Winchester cathedral

112 Left, Wolvesey Palace, Winchester. The main structure of the castle was built by Henry – one of his six castles

113 Right above, classical influence in twelfth century Winchester; a centaur on a late twelfth century capital

114 Right, the font of Tournai marble in Winchester cathedral: detail from the miracle of St Nicholas

115 Left above, St Paul
shakes the viper off his
hand at Melita;
Canterbury cathedral,
St Anselm's chapel, late
twelfth century

116 Left below, St Paul
blind and helpless after
his conversion; mosaic
in the Palatine chapel,
Palermo, mid-twelfth
century

117 Right above, the
death of the Virgin in
the Henry of Blois
Psalter, c. 1150–60
(see p. 149)

118 Right below, the
death of the Virgin in
the Chiesa della
Martorana, Palermo,
twelfth century

A constant fusion of local traditions with inspiration drawn from every part of the world and many segments of the surviving past characterized the art and the literature of the twelfth century. Thus we have seen Roman, Byzantine and Moslem idioms learned, transmitted and transmogrified in western art and architecture. If we ask in the end, was this the work of artists or of patrons? we shall wait till doomsday for the answer. No interim report will satisfy us if it does not recognize the peculiar importance of observant crusaders and of other patrons less adventurous but even more observant, like Suger and Henry of Blois; but we should be even more suspicious of any doctrine which undervalued the artistic sense and power to adapt of the master masons, sculptors and painters of the age. The originality and inventiveness of the twelfth century is hard to imagine without the work of men like Suger; without Theophilus and Gilbert and the craftsmen of Monreale and Winchester it could not have been conceived at all.

VI · GEOFFREY OF MONMOUTH
WALTER MAP AND
WOLFRAM VON ESCHENBACH

WOLFRAM AND TWELFTH CENTURY THEOLOGY

In this book we have tried to see the twelfth century renaissance as a movement with many centres and different modes of expression, but one whose modes were in a variety of ways interrelated. Scholars and poets flourished and multiplied; their art became richer and far more sophisticated. It can hardly be supposed that this was pure coincidence. Yet at first sight there must appear to be little connection between the school-room and the baronial hall, between the learned scholar like Abelard or John of Salisbury and Wolfram, the knight without formal education. Some links between the two worlds were hinted at in our first chapter (see p. 11); now we must turn to scrutinize more closely the territories in which some coexistence was possible between the love of God and courtly or romantic, human love, and between theology, history and fiction.

What links can we find between the Latin literature of the first half of the twelfth century and the vernacular epics of the early thirteenth ? The first and best example for our purpose is the *Willehalm* of Wolfram von Eschenbach. It was written about a decade after his more famous *Parzival*, that is to say in the 1210s; written by a poor German knight who claimed (with some exaggeration) to be illiterate; and yet it represents in a remarkable degree a theological insight and a sophistication of a kind wholly unthinkable a century earlier.

Willehalm stands in a close relation with two earlier verna-cular poems. To the French *chanson de geste*, *Guillaume d'Orange*

119 Wolfram von Eschenbach; from the famous Minnesinger manuscript of *c.* 1315

it owes the outline of its story; to the German version of the most famous of the *chansons de geste*, the *Rolandslied*, it was in some sort an answer, a riposte. Like all the romances of its age, it is full of fighting and of 'chivalry' (see p. 20). But in a positive sense it represents the struggle for expression, in a sensitive and religious mind of original cast, of the humane aspects of the theological movements of the twelfth century.

The story of *Willehalm*, in contrast to *Parzival*, is comparatively simple. Count William of Orange has carried off a pagan princess, Gyburg, and married her. The priests of her religion insist that her father and brothers and a large Saracen host be mobilized for her recapture. In the first battle the Christian army is entirely destroyed; only William escapes. He returns for a moment to his castle, then hastens north to seek further assistance, leaving Gyburg to stand the siege. William returns with an army gathered in the north, in the court of the French king, and in a second battle, after a great slaughter on both sides, the Saracens are beaten. One of the central themes of *Willehalm* makes explicit something which had been adumbrated in the final sections of *Parzival* some years before. After Parzival's triumph and succession to the throne of the Grail, he ceased to be the centre of the poem. The chief characters of the last books are his son Lohengrim, the knight of the Swan, who ultimately succeeds him; and his half-brother Feirefiz, the half-black son of the oriental consort of Gahmuret, Parzival's father. Feirefiz has his father's love of adventure and of women; he also has Parzival's essential purity and goodness of heart. He is eventually baptized; but even before this event he and his mother are held up to us as examples of natural goodness. The author of the *Rolandslied*, a clergyman writing about a generation earlier, had happily consigned the heathen to hell. The problem is not brought to a head in *Parzival*, but it is clearly there. Parzival himself, in considerable measure, had been saved by his own goodness and loyalty; if virtues such as these can save a Christian, what of the good heathen?

Gyburg herself, the Saracen wife of the Christian hero, has been baptized; but she retains a strong sympathy with her own family and people. The heathen too are God's handiwork. She pleads for them on this ground:

> hoert eins tumben wîbes rât,
> schônt der gotes handgetât.

'Hear the counsel of a simple woman, and spare God's handi-work.' Her attitude, and the whole problem, are underlined by the personality of Rennewart, a heathen prince who lives disguised as a royal scullion and is discovered to be Gyburg's brother as the result of his prowess in the final battle. *Willehalm* is unfinished; the baptism of Rennewart, which ought to be its climax, is never reached. It is the proper conclusion of the poem; but Wolfram has set himself the problem: 'What difference does it make?' – a problem to which he may well have had a clear answer; but it seems likely that he did not want to spoil his deeper question, of the Christian attitude to good pagans, by introducing this further problem, and so left the

157

great poem unfinished, has left it indeed with Rennewart missing and his fate wholly uncertain.

The theological issues sit clearly on the surface of *Willehalm*. It opens with a prayer, in which Wolfram's humble confidence in God is based on 'A sign you gave: you wore human form; and this sign confirms the tie and bond of kinship even to folk like me. My trust, my faith is renewed also by the rite of baptism.' Baptism, by which he could call himself a Christian, and so partake in Christ's name, was a token to him of special kinship; but there is a hint already, in the prologue, that God's providence is larger, is indeed immeasurable. Throughout the poem, in various forms, the problem of the heathen and their relation to Christians and to God is constantly being posed. It is not the only problem handled; but it is, I think, a problem of special interest to historians, because it is one of the most vivid and powerful pieces of evidence for the spread of serious moral enquiry deep and wide in the world of the early thirteenth century; because it reveals the influence of theological ideas, channelled doubtless through the clergy whom Wolfram met in the course of his life; and above all refutes the central theme of the *chansons de geste* and the crusading movement which they inspired. It is the most striking piece of evidence in its way for the failure of the crusading movement in the thirteenth century.

In the popular theology of the late eleventh and early twelfth centuries, still represented in the *Rolandslied*, the heathen were cattle for the slaughter. The Princess Anna Comnena, looking at the crusading hosts from the walls of Byzantium in 1096–7, felt as if she was witnessing another barbarian avalanche; it seemed as if all the riff-raff of the west had descended on Byzantium. And so, especially in the following of Peter the Hermit, a great part of it had. The crusade was the adventure of the hour, and the notion of a holy war, with an indulgence of unprecedented potency attached, made it immensely attractive. Motives were mixed from the start; but the central theme of the crusade made it a good subject for religious enthusiasm.

120, 121 The Song of Roland. In the manuscript, above, Archbishop Turpin and the king (Charlemagne) are on the left; in the relief, below, Roland himself is on the right (both twelfth century)

122 St James, as slayer of the Moors; from the tympanum in his cathedral, Santiago de Compostela, second half of the twelfth century

The decline of crusading fervour came slowly but surely in the course of the twelfth and thirteenth centuries. Many reasons have been found for it. One powerful reason was the growth of a new attitude to the Moslem. Responsible churchmen had always maintained that it was better to convert the Moslem than to kill him; and steps were taken in Spain by enlightened men like Peter the Venerable, abbot of Cluny, to investigate the nature of Islam and to hold debates with educated Moslems. The idea of converting the Moslem bore little fruit; but the idea was current in the early thirteenth century, and was an important part of the platform of St Francis of Assisi, who himself preached before Moslem leaders in Syria in the years following the completion of *Willehalm*.

Wolfram's sympathy with the heathen was not due to any understanding of Islam. He reveals himself as ignorant as most Christians of the elements of Mohammed's faith; and he speaks as if Gyburg and her relatives were good in spite of, certainly not because of, their religion. His sympathy comes from two sources: first, growing contact between Christian and Moslem on the frontiers of Christendom, in the Holy Land, in Syria, throughout the Mediterranean, above all, in Sicily and Spain, which bred a new respect between the races, a respect which could filter through to other parts of Europe where there were men prepared to consider such tolerance; and secondly, it was not unrelated to theological trends in the contemporary schools. It is impossible to tell precisely how much he knew of formal theology, and fairly certain that he had no direct contact with the seminal books of the twelfth century theologians. But he was certainly aware of changing ideas, as an observant, reflective and pious man who rubbed shoulders with learned clerics was likely to be. The doctrine of predestination, which dominates the thought of *Parzival*, had dominated too the theological world of the tenth and eleventh centuries. God was a distant potentate, all-seeing, all-powerful: a father and a judge. There was room for human free will, but precious little; and no room for human merit. The eleventh and twelfth centuries saw the birth of new currents in theology as in every sphere of life and thought. Most conspicuously, they saw the birth of a new interest in the human Jesus; a new devotion to him and a new concern with all the circumstances of his life. The cult of the human Jesus, so closely linked in its origin to the desire to see his earthly home in Palestine and with the crusading ideals, came to a height when the crusading ideal was already on the wane, in Wolfram's contemporary St Francis of Assisi, most human and humane of the medieval saints, the saint, furthermore, who made popular the Christmas crib. Jesus came to be viewed more and more as a human being, not by the exclusion of his divine nature, but by the restoration of a balance strangely lacking in the notions of earlier centuries.

To the doctrine that the heathen were cattle the Church at large had never subscribed; but the Church had never held out any hope of salvation for the heathen, nor, in the eleventh century, for the majority of Christians. Wolfram's doctrine, that God will not punish a man for ignorance, has won assent in almost every branch of the Christian Church; his other doctrine, that a pagan who leads a good life not merely may receive, but merits God's grace, savours of Pelagianism – of

the heresy *par excellence* of the intelligent Christian layman, that what a man makes of his life matters more than the inscrutable foreknowledge of God. None the less, though in some ways unorthodox, though in many ways exceptional, Wolfram's ideas represent to us in a revealing way what happened when an intelligent layman set about reverently to follow out the teaching of orthodox churchmen about God's love and man's response. He lived in a world where there were increasing numbers of laymen – knights, merchants and artisans in particular – ready and eager to pursue new religious ideas and practices. Often this took the form of heresy, and the late twelfth century saw the escalation of heretical movements in many parts of Europe, especially in southern France and northern Italy; but it was often orthodox, at least in intention, as was the imaginative scheme of St Francis and his followers to bridge the gap between learned clerics and the humble and poor laity by founding an Order of friars which was in origin neither learned nor in the main clerical.

123 Far Left, St Peter
baptizing; from Roger's
altar (see p. 107)

124 Left, the conversion
of a Jewish boy; from a
thirteenth century
window in Le Mans
cathedral

Francis and Wolfram were contemporaries; both drew
much inspiration from current notions of chivalry. But they
knew nothing of one another directly, so far as we can tell,
and it would be quite false to picture Wolfram as a Franciscan
manqué. He was a knight, and proud of it; and in the end his
strongest claim on the interest of the historian is as an exponent
of chivalry. The link between *Parzival* and the Latin literature
of the twelfth century renaissance is more complex than that
between *Willehalm* and its theology, yet just as much worth
tracing. Parzival's career – even more that of the second hero
of the poem, Gawain – was lived in and out of the court of
Artus, of King Arthur; and its central purpose was the pursuit
of the Grail. Both take us to the heart of the legend-making
of the twelfth century, the formation of the Matter of Britain,
on French soil, with materials drawn from all over the Celtic
world – perhaps one should say from all over the known
world – and above all from the creative imagination of a small
group of great story-tellers.

125 Wolfram preaching tolerance; from a manuscript of
Willehalm of *c.* 1250–75

WOLFRAM AND
ST FRANCIS OF ASSISI

126 St Francis, Wolfram's contemporary, surrounded by scenes
from his life: the bottom left panel shows him before the
Sultan; in that immediately above it he is preaching to the
birds. An early Florentine painting (*c.* 1250), now in the
Bardi Chapel in Santa Croce, Florence

'Arthur is he', wrote William of Malmesbury, the English historian, in the 1120s, 'of whom the Breton ditties still burble; but he was worthy, not to be dreamed of in lying tales, but to be honoured in true histories, as one who long sustained his failing land and urged on the inhabitants' unbroken spirits to battle.'[39] Early in 1139, while travelling in Normandy, another well-known English chronicler of the age, Henry, archdeacon of Huntingdon, was delighted to discover just such a 'true history': a Latin chronicle which provided him with a full account of King Arthur and of much else besides, going back into the mists of time; filling the notorious gaps in British history, making possible a new and much improved edition of his own *Historia Anglorum*. Already, or soon after, the 'true history' received an epilogue, in which the author renounces any intention of carrying the story forward from the seventh century.

> The kings who have ruled in Wales from that time I leave as a theme for Caradoc of Llancarvan, my contemporary, and those of the Saxons for William of Malmesbury and Henry of Huntingdon: but I forbid them to say anything of the kings of the Britons, since they have not that book written in Breton which Walter archdeacon of Oxford brought out of Brittany; which is a true account of their history; and which I have thus in these princes' honour taken pains to translate into Latin.

Thus Geoffrey of Monmouth is traditionally supposed the founder of the Arthurian cycle of legends, though it is commonly said today that his influence has been much exaggerated. Arthur was honoured in Breton ditties, and over an area far wider than Brittany, before Geoffrey wrote; and the material in his book is only a small part of the rich vein of legend quarried by the authors of the courtly romances of the late twelfth century. It is true that source material was copious, once the romancers began to look for it. Geoffrey's claim to our attention, however, is not as a quarry, but in the fact that his book and the poems of Chrétien of Troyes, the most distinguished French poet of the next generation, had an exceptionally powerful literary influence. Geoffrey was influential because he told marvellous stories, about King Lear and Cymbeline and above all about Arthur, dressed up as 'true history'; he made Arthur respectable in the best circles; and he did so because he was himself a Celt – probably a Breton brought up in Wales – who cared for Celtic traditions; an Anglo-Norman with a feel for the cosmopolitan cultural world of the Anglo-Norman aristocracy; and a cleric capable of writing – or at least of parodying in the most convincing fashion – in the best serious historical manner of the age. Plagiarism was a respectable art, and Geoffrey himself quarried freely; but he made no attempt to place his discoveries in their true context, and a great deal of what is best in his work was frankly fictitious. Walter, archdeacon of Oxford, was real enough, and no doubt Geoffrey's accomplice; but the Breton book never existed. Caradoc was a notable author of saints' lives of little or no historical value. Clearly Geoffrey was pulling his leg; and it is probable that Henry of Huntingdon – an archdeacon in the same diocese (of Lincoln) as Walter – was a selected victim; it is otherwise incredible that Henry should have had to travel to Normandy to make his first acquaintance with a book composed on his own doorstep.

HISTORY: WILLIAM OF MALMESBURY AND EADMER

The reference to William of Malmesbury may well be a half-serious bow to the most distinguished historian of the age, and a man to whom Geoffrey had already paid the compliment of imitation. The word *Historia* meant 'history' or 'story', and it is often said that the two were not clearly distinguished in this age. This is not wholly true. The purpose of history was to edify, to instruct, to answer men's curiosity, and to entertain; and William himself took pains to throw in a good story here and there in his own histories in case his readers should nod. But he was a true historian, in the tradition of Bede, keen and well-equipped to reconstruct the past. Some of the best historical writing of the Middle Ages was not at all of this character (see p. 71). The most notable exponent of the alternative, that of contemporary history, in the generation before John was Eadmer, the Canterbury monk whose life and outlook were dominated by his love for his cathedral and for his archbishop, St Anselm. The climate of the late eleventh century, the intense personal experience of his meeting with Anselm and his discipleship, combined with no mean talent as an author and a scribe to produce one of the most original biographies of the Middle Ages, made famous by Professor Southern's book *St Anselm and his Biographer*. His aim, like that of most medieval biographers, was to make his audience remember, admire and revere his hero; but he had no wish to place him in a stained glass window – he introduces us to him, face to face, at his most characteristic, in his conversation. No doubt this is not *verbatim* reporting; but it is of the essence of Eadmer's method that he reconstructs a conversation, as near as may be, using Anselm's words and images and characteristic modes of expression. It is the first, and in many ways the best, of a kind of intimate biography which was to be characteristic of the twelfth and early thirteenth centuries, but unusual at other times in the Middle Ages.

Eadmer's other chief work, the *History of Recent Events*, was equally inspired by Anselm, and its main theme is the public career of the saint as archbishop of Canterbury. It contains Eadmer's account of his relations with William Rufus and Henry I, and gems of conversation between the talkative Anselm and the brief, staccato, explosive, stuttering Rufus. Eadmer shows little interest in earlier history. In contrast William of Malmesbury was at his best in dealing with the past; for he had the research student's flair. He lacked critical sense and failed to distinguish genuine from forged even though he lived in an age when forgers flourished, as he must have known. But he could reconstruct the history of a monastery from an untidy pile of charters; and he had the sense and zeal to pursue his enquiries carefully but sensibly. As with Bede himself, or as with Eadmer, history was only one of his interests; saints' life and Biblical commentaries were also part of his repertoire. Late in life he turned his hand to contemporary history, and his own *Historia Novella* is certainly very readable though partial and prejudiced like most of its kind. But his fame rests on his *History of the English Bishops*, in which the story of every see is disentangled from Bede's day to his own; and the *History of the English Kings*, which provided Geoffrey of Monmouth with the inspiration for his *History of the British Kings*. It inspired him by showing him how one should write if one wanted to be taken seriously; and it may be that William's suggestion that Arthur deserved a place in true histories inspired him directly to his effort to give him one.

127 Eadmer's handwriting; the opening of his *Historia Novorum* (*History of Recent Events*)

But if Geoffrey first floated Arthur as a respectable subject for serious discourse, he invented neither the Round Table nor the Holy Grail, for these are conspicuously absent from his book. The origin of the Grail is a quagmire in which many scholarly reputations have sunk without trace. In general, the Grail comes, like Arthur, from the mists of earlier legend – though only the very bold can assert with confidence whether the legend was originally Celtic or oriental – and was adapted and altered to suit the tastes and needs of numerous romancers. It took many different forms; but of these four are especially worth study. If you like a light and airy tale of adventure, with a strong mysterious core, never properly explained, then Chrétien's *Conte du Graal* will suit you; if you wish to study the Grail as an example of medieval mysticism, the thirteenth century *Queste del saint Graal* (in which Sir Percival the Welshman has been overtaken by Sir Galahad) is the thing; if you wish to see the Grail against the background of great music, you will go to Bayreuth for Wagner's *Parsifal*; if you wish to hear a great story superbly told, take Wolfram's – and it is undoubtedly one of the most exciting entries into the mind of a layman, formally uneducated yet sophisticated by the literary traditions of the twelfth century renaissance.

The author of the *Queste*, writing interminable French prose in the 1220s (or thereabouts),[40] claimed that the *Queste* – and its sequel, the *Mort Artu* – were translations, from a Latin original preserved at the abbey of Salisbury (which never existed), made 'by Walter Map at the request of King Henry his lord'. It is quite certain that he did nothing of the kind, almost equally certain that there was good reason to attribute a version of the Grail story to Walter, for these little pseudo-historical references in the romances are intended to pretend truth while stating palpable fiction – and yet to tickle the fancy by including some plausible element of near-truth. This kind of reference is an echo of Geoffrey's claim to have translated the Breton book supplied by another Walter, also, like Map, archdeacon of Oxford. We shall probably never know the answer to this fascinating mystery, but we may take it as likely that Walter Map, as well as being a highly respectable archdeacon in the diocese over which St Hugh of Lincoln presided (1186–1200), also moved in the circles in which courtly romances were being planned and executed.

The only surviving work which can reasonably be attributed to him, however, is that extraordinary jumble, the *De nugis curialium*, Courtiers' Trifles. Among the many stories scattered about in this book, there is a brief heroic legend concerning Gado and Offa, which is a remarkable parody, or imitation, of Geoffrey of Monmouth's fictitious history by a man who evidently knew how Geoffrey had worked. Roman roads, Stonehenge, and the ruins of Caerleon-on-Usk inspired Geoffrey to some of his wilder flights of fancy; and Gado and Offa were evidently inspired by Wat's and Offa's dykes on the frontiers of England and Wales. Offa married the daughter of a Roman emperor, for 'many such unions between Romans and Britons are recorded'; and the mixture of bravado and pillaging from sources probable and improbable, used to construct a better story than any of its precursors, would suggest Geoffrey's inspiration, even without the direct echoes which establish it. The most famous example of Map's skill in reworking traditional material is in the tract embedded in *De nugis* dissuading a friend from marriage. He takes a little story from Cicero, with frills from Quintilian and names from Aulus Gellius; and here is the result:

Pacuvius, weeping, said to his neighbour Arrius, 'Friend, I have a disastrous tree in my garden: my first wife hung herself on it, so did my second later on, and now my third has done the same.' Said Arrius; 'I wonder that after so many strokes of luck you find it in you to weep.' And again, 'Good gods, what expenses has that tree suspended for you!' And a third time; 'Friend, give me some cuttings of that tree to plant.'

In one or two of his stories, Map reveals an interest in the themes of the courtly romances, though no sympathy at all with 'courtly' or 'romantic' love. His story of Sadius and Galo is an essay in this genre, brilliantly skilful, satirical, and thoroughly unpleasant. It is of great interest in the history of literature because it reveals to us a little of the mechanics of the influence of the classical renaissance on the themes of contemporary vernacular literature. It has often been disputed whether courtly love was the fruit of Arabian influence from Spain, or of Ovid, or of Ovid misunderstood, or of Christian mysticism, or whether it was a native growth in the vineyards of Provence, spreading apace as the century went on into the regions of Claret, Burgundy and Champagne. It becomes increasingly clear that it was all these things; that both its roots and its own nature are far more complex and sophisticated than an earlier tradition of patronizing criticism would allow. In Sadius and Galo, Map shows us how a great exponent of the art of the short story could use materials and themes largely provided by Terence and Ovid. Galo is a knight who falls in love with a lady and in the end they live together happily; so far a normal romantic tale. But Map interweaves with this an inversion, not to say perversion, of the rules of the romance: instead of the knight pursuing the lady, it is the lady (in Map's story, to make matters worse, a queen) who develops a passion for a knight and attempts to indulge it. The two themes are united in the person of Galo, who is the knight pursuant of the first, traditional story, the knight pursued of the second, inverted romance; Sadius is the friend who tries to put off the queen by a somewhat crude device.

Map's book was read, so far as we know, by almost no one in its own day. It is not therefore for its influence that it concerns us, but as an indication, a kind of thermometer of the temperature of the age. Sadius and Galo indicate the links between classical sources and the developed romance; and it is no accident that some of the characteristics of Galo's queen reappear in the Isolde of Gottfried von Strassburg. Gado and

128 Terence; a scene from the *Andria*, twelfth century. His plays had an influence on Map's technique of dialogue

Offa indicate the relation of history and fiction – and elsewhere in the book there are extended passages of semi-fictitious history, not intended to deceive, but intended to parody contemporary historical writing: a sort of twelfth century *1066 and all that*. The immediate interest of these is that they would have no point if the two genres of history and fiction were not clearly in principle distinguished, but in practice confused. A historian's business, as the Venerable Bede had laid it down, was not to state what had actually happened, but faithfully to relate the story passed on to him. In practice, Bede himself knew well that some of the stories were mistaken, and he resolved this, either (in the case of Eddius' life of Wilfrid) by leaving dubious matter out, or (with the sagas describing the baptism of Edwin) by putting divergent narratives end to

173

end. But men like William of Malmesbury reckoned that history involved three things: investigation, craftsmanship, and good story telling; and this could involve them in honest invention. The conventions decreed, for example, that dialogue should be included, which the historian was expected to invent. William was an honest man, though not unprejudiced; Geoffrey of Monmouth a thoroughly dishonest man, though it may be doubted if his purpose was very serious. Some, like Eadmer, could be both. In all that he said about the person of Anselm, he was scrupulous, for this was a subject which invoked a historian's dedication to truth as he saw it. In much of what he said of the privileges of the archbishop of Canterbury, he lied; and after Anselm's death he condoned forgery for what he supposed a sacred cause. Many factors went to make this one of the great ages of literary forgery, and of the forgery of documents. Written testimony was coming to play an entirely new role as legal evidence for title to properties and privileges. In England, the Norman Conquest had provided both a chaos in tenures and the means to resolve it. The twelfth century renaissance provided the necessary interest and skill in craftsmanship, both literary and metallurgical – for forgery of documents involved forgery of seals and seal matrices as well.

There is, however, an interesting and significant shift in the making of documents, which helps to explain why forgery, along with so many of the Latin and scholarly movements of the twelfth century, petered out in the concentration and specialization of thought of the thirteenth century. Eadmer, Orderic and William of Malmesbury are known to us as craftsmen in handwriting as well as in Latin prose; this tradition enjoyed a curious St Luke's summer in Matthew Paris in the thirteenth century. But, broadly speaking, we do not expect to have autograph books for men like John of Salisbury or St Bernard or Walter Map, because they used secretaries. Craftsmanship became a professional thing, and the art of forgery first passed into the hands of professional improvers of muniments in the late twelfth century and then declined.

Yet in spite of the confusion into which contemporary attitudes and pressing practical needs might throw them, most students of history and fiction in the twelfth century saw clearly enough that they were different modes of expression, and that for a simple and obvious reason, since the chief role of the most fashionable mode of literature was precisely to invert, to parody, to play tricks with ordinary human experience. The chief model of the early twelfth century was the French epic, the *chanson de geste*; and however absurd, the *chanson* was a plain tale of war, and so had much the same content as many a warring chronicle; confusion was possible, and one quite often finds books which combine the roles not too uncomfortably, and not only books, since the Bayeux Tapestry itself seems closely related to both.[41] But in the romances of Arthur's and Alexander's courts which conquered the Anglo-French world and then the German in the mid and late twelfth century the central theme is courtly love (see p. 20). Courtly love meant the slavish service of a woman by a man in a world where, notoriously, it was the woman who was the slave of male modes of conduct, of the marriage market and the marriage bed. Most of this literature would have been impossible if its authors had had any idea of describing society as they saw it.

It is sometimes implied that the cult of courtly love involved the authors of the romances in certain strict beliefs: that love was the mainspring of action; that love must be unrequited, at least in a physical sense; that love and marriage were incompatible; that in so far as courtly love was a carnal thing, it glorified adultery. This line of belief is the invention of *Geistes-geschichte*, a form of study to which we owe much genuine understanding, but which has the tendency to urge us to believe that the outlook of our forefathers was far more uniform and monolithic than the evidence suggests. But it seems to me, quite simply, that every one of the really notable, and really influential, authors of romances saw either the ironies and contradictions of courtly love, or condemned it out of hand. The greatest of the French romancers, Chrétien of Troyes, plays the irony and the romance with a subtlety and obscurity akin to Shakespeare's; to suppose that he idealizes courtly love is as absurd as to read *Romeo and Juliet* as a straight 'romantic' play. In his *Cligès*, the lightest of his major poems, he shows among other things that he did not misunderstand Ovid. Early in the poem a young man and a maiden put to sea, chaperoned by the queen. The poet gives us a long and ironical account of the activities of Love, of Cupid with his darts; then tells how sick the two became; yet the queen (the poet tells us, enlarging a trick suggested by Ovid) put it all down to sea-sickness. In his *Lancelot* Chrétien shows his insight into the meaning of courtly love at its most refined in the famous scene when Lancelot faces what was reckoned at the time the supreme disgrace of travelling in a cart on the way to rescue his lady. He hesitates, only for a moment; but for that hesitation, that hint that his devotion is not all-consuming, the lady makes him pay. The payment made, however, he has his reward; he has made his pilgrimage, he worships at the shrine; and with a delicacy which is not at all calculated to hide the basic point, Chrétien shows to what the cult of courtly love tends when he reveals Lancelot treating as a saint's shrine the bed in which he has just committed adultery with Queen Guinevere.

GOTTFRIED VON STRASSBURG'S 'TRISTAN'

Both the ironic play with the theme of Love, or Cupid, and the comparison of courtly love with the cult of the saints, are brought to a climax in the *Tristan* of Gottfried von Strassburg. One of the most striking episodes in the poem is the scene of Tristan and Isolde's life together in the Cave of Lovers, which is in many respects modelled on an early Gothic cathedral –

176

129 Tristan; a German manuscript of the first half of the thirteenth century. King Mark and Isolde; Isolde and Tristan sleeping with a sword between them; Isolde swears to her innocence ▶

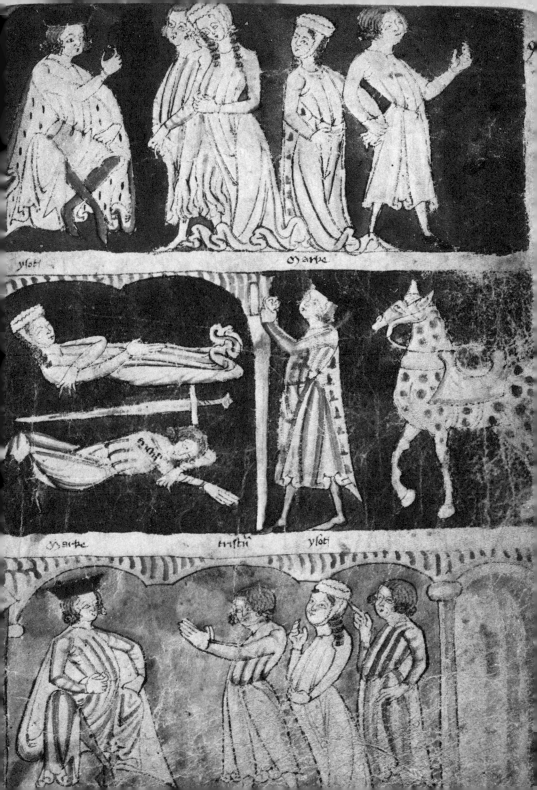

ysoſt   Marſe

Marſe   triſtũ   ysoſt

with the shrine, the crystalline bed at its centre, and its proportions carefully calculated to symbolize Love's cult. There are many surviving versions of the story: in virtually all, Tristan and Isolde are united in undying love by a magic potion, although Isolde is married to King Mark. Most of them have this in common, that they reveal a full awareness that there is nothing necessarily romantic about the hero and heroine's predicament; that courtly love tended to produce a blasphemous parody of contemporary Christian attitudes; and the more subtle reveal some insight into the genuine human problems which romantic love and marriage can create in any age.

Gottfried's poem has a wonderfully smooth finish, and some critics have supposed that Isolde is meant to be a romantic figure. She is not, of course, a character in the modern sense: she is a woman who exists only in the poem, and so only in relation to a certain situation, and this is emphasized by the fact that she starts by hating Tristan, and is only won to love him by a pure accident and a magical intervention. After that, she has no command over her feeling towards him. How romantic a figure she is in Gottfried's exposition may be deduced from the following events. First, once she has enjoyed sleeping with Tristan there is a difficulty about her marriage to King Mark, which she overcomes by bribing her faithful lady in waiting (who is still a virgin) to spend part of the first night with Mark: Isolde is then in panic because of Brangane's hold over her, and arranges for the lady's murder, being prevented only by accident. In case one is inclined to attribute Isolde's murderous quality wholly to her special circumstance, Gottfried had already treated his reader to a scene in which she attempted to murder Tristan before she loved him. After her marriage to Mark, her life is increasingly dedicated to a pretty mixture of pretence, spleen and hypocrisy. Her life becomes a powerful comment, whatever Gottfried's own views may have been, on the power of Love uncontrolled by human will, because administered in a magic potion.

The *Parzival* of Wolfram von Eschenbach owes much of its essential material to the *Perceval* (the *Conte du Graal*) of Chrétien of Troyes; but at the end Wolfram tells us that Chrétien had got the story wrong, and he, Wolfram, took the true story from Kyot the Provençal, who had translated it from the Arabic. Thus Wolfram acknowledged his debt to Geoffrey of Monmouth and poked fun at Gottfried von Strassburg. It is very unlikely that he knew Geoffrey of Monmouth at first hand; but just as in *Willehalm* he reveals some of the most inspired insights of twelfth century theology, so in his *Parzival* he had already gathered a rich harvest in literary themes with which to display his views on the code of chivalry and courtly love. Thus he summarized many of the glories of the world of Arthurian romance of which Geoffrey was the main founder, and he invented Kyot and his Arabian source as a counter to Chrétien, and a parody of Gottfried, whose respect for his source, his *auctoritas*, was much greater than Wolfram's. In a similar way Geoffrey had invented his Breton source to make fun of Henry of Huntingdon and all the world.

Parzival's father, Gahmuret the Angevin, was a bold, adventurous knight, who roamed both occident and orient, married and then deserted a Moslem wife, and after remarrying in the west Herzeloyde, Parzival's mother, went off to more adventure and to death. Herzeloyde determined to bring up her son in ignorance of chivalry, so that he would not suffer his father's fate. But God's predestinating will was too strong for her, and the first part of the poem shows predestination operating through what would appear to the modern reader to be fate and heredity. Heredity is an important symbol in Wolfram, not because he had studied genetics, but because it enabled him to reveal predestination in an artistic way. Parzival, for all his mother's care, grows up a dare-devil knight errant like his father. A slight carelessness on his part (venial at the human level) leads his mother to die of a broken heart

because she thinks he is deserting her; a slight attack of cove-
tousness leads him to despoil a knight he has killed; rigid
adherence to a mistaken code of manners leads him not to
ask his host in a strange castle after his health. Trivial things in
themselves, but when related to an all-powerful divine predestination, fearful in their consequences.

Parzival's host in the strange castle, unknown to him,
was his uncle Anfortas, king of the Grail, doomed to an
appalling suffering until such time as his nephew shall come and
ask the simple question 'Oeheim, waz wirret dier?' – 'Uncle
what ails you?' God has not willed that Parzival see the Grail
yet; and so he must toil and struggle for five years more before
the story has its end.

For five years Parzival's quest continues, until one day he
meets the hermit Trevrizent, Anfortas' brother, and so also
uncle to Parzival. Trevrizent and Parzival hold a long conference together; it is the central scene of the poem, and the
skill with which Parzival's sins and misunderstandings are
gradually unveiled, and the two come to recognize each other,
is one of Wolfram's greatest achievements. Parzival makes
confession to Trevrizent (though he is a layman) and receives
absolution; from now on God is with him, and he can go to the
Grail castle, ask his question, relieve Anfortas, and succeed
him as king without more ado.

This is a very jejune summary of an immensely rich and
complex story. Of its many complexities and points of interest
two particularly demand our attention. The first is that
the poem contains an exceedingly elaborate searching out
of all that was involved in the code of chivalry. My summary
has left out the story of Gawain, which occupies nearly half
the book, and is in relation to chivalry equally important to
Parzival's. Wolfram could see many of the follies and absurdi-
ties of chivalry; he did not admire it in all its forms, but only
the higher, idealized chivalry symbolized by the Grail. He
was a knight, and proud of it. In the end, the supreme virtue
which Parzival displays is loyalty, *triuwe*, the specific virtue

130 Parzival and Feirefiz (see p. 157); from a German manuscript of *c.* 1250 ▶

of the knight. We are shown *triuwe* in three settings: in relation to God, to man and to marriage. It is made clear that God's decision to favour Parzival after his confession was not a whim; that God led Parzival to Trevrizent's hermitage, in part at least, because Parzival had earned it. He had earned it, not by faith, but by *triuwe*; by stubborn loyalty he conquered doubt and despair, and these (in the eyes of Wolfram's God) earn a man grace.

Triuwe among men is so constant a theme that one can only appreciate it by reading the poem; and the more one reads of *Parzival*, the more one marvels to see the human values of worlds so diverse as those of Abelard, St Bernard and the *chansons de geste* providing the recipes for a single rich and varied feast. The largest ingredient is chivalry, fictitious and actual, and together with the varieties of knightly behaviour, in the saddle, the tournament field and the dining hall, we meet the varieties of human love, displayed with a remarkable and often bewildering mixture of savagery and tolerance. As exponents of knightly *triuwe* and its accompaniments, Parzival and Gawain have much in common; in the pursuit of love they are quite different.

Parzival was married before he went on his first visit to the Grail castle; and his *triuwe* to his wife is one of his outstanding qualities. It is a love stronger and more profound than courtly love, and the contrast is noted in a variety of ways. In spite of five years of separation, Parzival's love for his wife is never in doubt; and reunion with his wife and children is the supreme reward of his final success. Wolfram seems to be saying as follows: the special duty of a Christian knight is fidelity, to himself, to his wife and family, and to God; then to his lord, to his followers, his comrades, to his order and his code; his calling is to show *triuwe* in every human situation.

One has only to compare the working out of loyalty in *Parzival* with its splendid but crude portrayal in the *Song of Roland* to see how large an injection has been made even into the world of ideas of an uneducated knight. Roland is still essentially barbaric, while Parzival, though showing many barbaric elements, is essentially civilized.

Yet Wolfram is above all the symbol of the variety of his age: the age of the Cathars, of St Francis, of courtly literature both sensual and ascetic. Courtly love, whatever its origin, was no easy yoke-fellow for the twelfth century Church, naturally suspicious of the excesses of human love and human pleasure; and it is very striking that it should have been a layman who first found the reconciliation between the two. He idealized married love; rejoiced whole-heartedly in earthly, human pleasures; and yet found a place for the other-worldliness and the asceticism of the Church. But it was the variety, not the reconciliation, which struck deepest root in the late twelfth and early thirteenth centuries; and we shall never understand or appreciate the twelfth century renaissance if we look constantly for common denominators and universal opinions. For it opened men's minds and broadened their vision.

131 Baptism of Feirefiz; from the Parzival manuscript of c. 1250

VII EPILOGUE

THE END OF THE TWELFTH CENTURY RENAISSANCE

The broadening vision of the twelfth century renaissance was short-lived. Much of what has been described in this book changed or decayed soon after 1200. Much, but not all. Only a generation separates the death of Wolfram from the birth of Dante; not more than two the death of Wolfram from the birth of Petrarch. In some spheres and in some places a sharp breach between the renaissance of the twelfth and of the fifteenth centuries makes nonsense of both movements. In Italy the first renaissance made less of a ripple on the stream of culture than in France; and this partly because the influence of the classical world was always nearer to hand, the sense of the Roman past more immediate than elsewhere; partly, it must be owned, because in certain respects Italy had less than her share of the revival. It is a false view of culture and of history which claims that nothing new arose in Italy in the fifteenth century – self-evidently one of the most creative milieux in man's recorded experience. Yet the search for origins has taken some scholars back from the fifteenth to the thirteenth century, and some have even claimed St Francis as a precursor of the Renaissance. This is, perhaps, mere word-play; yet the truth which lies behind it is that there is a certain continuity, visible in the monuments of Italy and in late medieval literature, from the classical world through the medieval, and through the vernacular literature of the thirteenth and fourteenth centuries, to the *Quattrocento*. Only a trained eye, or a mind well versed in Baedeker, can distinguish in the Baptistery at Florence, or in San Clemente at Rome, what in the design, the inspiration and the finished work of art represents the late Roman world and what the Romanesque; and Italian Romanesque long survived the Gothic conquest of France, to help lay the foundations of the new styles of the Renaissance. Italian Gothic was assuredly more than an intrusion or an episode; yet there is a sense in which in art and architecture, in the late Middle Ages, Rome had her revenge on Alaric.

In the twelfth century Latin and vernacular literature grew and flourished together. In the thirteenth vernacular literature, in many parts of Europe, went on to further triumphs. But Latin literature, for a time, decayed. The decadence of the twelfth century renaissance, if such it should be called, was a literary decadence; as the horizons widened, some of the idioms in which new ideas and new artistic creation had been expressed were lost or became hidden. At the same time, the widening of the horizons, in that as in other ages, drove men to specialize; and just as specialization is the condition of intellectual advance, so it tends – or has tended in man's recorded past – to stifle imaginative, creative impulses. At the turn of the twelfth and thirteenth centuries, Stephen Langton could compose highly technical Biblical commentaries, a moving hymn, and inspire *Magna Carta*; a little later the German Jordan of Saxony could compose legislation more sophisticated than *Magna Carta* (in his additions to the *Constitutions* of the Dominican Order) and write some of the most vivid Latin letters of the age. At a lower level, Matthew Paris, a conservative member of a conservative community, reproduced the range of accomplishments of the monk-scholars of an earlier age: he was chronicler, hagiographer, scribe and artist rolled into one. Yet most students of the twelfth and thirteenth centuries are struck by the contrast between the experimental, diverse Latin of the earlier schools and the dried, shrivelled, mechanically perfect Latin of the great scholastics, between the range of interests and studies of the age of Abelard, and the specialization of the world of St Thomas Aquinas.

This is a selective book, and I can only hope to illustrate three ways in which the twelfth century renaissance may be reckoned to have contained within it the seeds of its own decay – three aspects of the renaissance of which little has been said.

First of all, the late twelfth and early thirteenth centuries witnessed the formal crystallization of the greater schools into universities, and the deliberate foundation of universities intended from the start to have special academic privileges. The title *magister* came to be confined (in learned circles) to men who had earned a licence to teach from the Chancellor, or his equivalent, in a recognized university; and this presupposed a course of many years' duration with a specific and rigorous content. Even in the Italian universities, first formed and fashioned by guilds of students, the power of the professors increased. For the next few centuries the authority of experienced academics – or moderately experienced, for a professor over forty was a rare antique in a medieval university – was reckoned of more account for the essential purposes of a university than the charisma of the student throng; and yet the most hardened academic must admit that much was lost when the first rapture of walking or riding hundreds of miles to sit at Abelard's feet was converted into the formal, structured course of thirteenth century Paris. A generation bred on syllabuses can hardly understand the inspiration of the medieval schools in their prime.

The most obvious failure of learned men in the twelfth century, perhaps, was to recover any knowledge of Greek imaginative literature. In part, this may be attributed to accidental causes. Although the movements of this book all presuppose a multitude of people prepared to listen and enjoy, the number of original minds was never great; and the number of men earnestly engaged in trying to discover lost works of ancient learning was always few. The basis of early twelfth century thought was Platonic; yet all of Plato that was known at first hand was the *Timaeus*; and all the century could add to the genuine corpus were translations of the *Phaedo* and *Meno* by Henry Aristippus, archdeacon of Catania. Sicily was a natural point of contact between the new western learning and the

Greek world; it also formed a link between Christendom and Islam, and in Sicily, Spain and the Near East western scholars could find treasures of ancient learning in Arabic disguise. Some of them visited Greece itself, and Byzantium. Yet it was only slowly that new works were translated, and knowledge of Greek in the west advanced hardly at all. The stamp of western interest in Greek and Arab literature in this period was set by the first of the great translators of the twelfth century, Adelard of Bath, who not only gave Euclid to the west, but a substantial store besides of Greek and Arabic science. Something of Aristotle was already known from the versions and commentaries of Boethius; to this were added, first the rest of his logical and metaphysical writings, then (in the late twelfth century) his scientific works; and finally, in the mid-thirteenth, the *Politics*.

Thus the work of translation was slow and painful, and it may be that Homer and Euripides never struck the attention or imagination of the translators; clearly their zest for Aristotle helped to preserve them from being charmed by the poets. But this can hardly be the whole explanation for their neglect. Homer at least was still read in Byzantium; and Aristotle's *Poetics* were translated along with the rest. They can have been little regarded, however, and seem to have aroused almost no curiosity about the literature they analyzed. In part this was no doubt due to the aversion of twelfth century Christians to anything in the shape of a play. Liturgical drama was respectable; secular drama a work of the devil. There were men in the twelfth century, as in most ages, to whom all secular learning was anathema; but in general, in spite of the quantity of propaganda against the pagan classics which was available in the works of the fathers, this sort of attitude impinged on the practice of twelfth century scholars only in a small measure. The most notable exception to this is that there was no revival of the classical theatre. Yet men like John of Salisbury read and admired the plays of Terence, and might have enjoyed Aristophanes; that they would have appreciated the tragedians is more doubtful. What seems hardly doubtful is that the *Iliad* and the *Odyssey* would have answered to many of the most brilliant and inventive impulses of the century; and Homer's neglect remains a puzzle. Or rather, perhaps, it serves to underline the thin stream of intellectual contact with the Greek world, and the scientific and metaphysical preoccupation of the chief translators.

It was not that imaginative literature went unregarded. No medium defines the rise and fall of the movement here described more precisely or more piquantly than the secular Latin lyric. Latin verses of various kinds had been written in almost every century: classroom hexameters and the like, at their best moving expressions of sentiment, most commonly religious sentiment, at their worst humdrum exercises; religious poems of various patterns, many deriving from quiet, rhythmic, lyrical meters mastered by the hymn writers of the age of the fathers. The hymn and sequences inspired twelfth century authors with the idea that there was a far wider range of music in the genius of the Latin tongue than classical lyric writers had been prepared to explore; and they were further encouraged to this thought by the rise of the vernacular lyric in the late eleventh and early twelfth centuries, first in Provence, then throughout France, and finally in many parts of western Europe. To the old question, was the Latin lyric based on the Provençal, or vice versa? there is no answer; they grew together. But if they lived in the same nest, the vernacular lyric proved in the end a cuckoo's child, for it went on growing through the thirteenth century while the Latin lyric rapidly died. This was partly because the other fledgling could do all that was wanted by the poets; partly because of the general decline in Latin literature in the thirteenth century; partly, perhaps, because the lyric poets exhausted a particular vein of ore, and failed to explore further. But in general it is a symptom of the change we have been trying to grasp and define in these last pages; and it is an outstanding example of the brief glories of the renaissance.

Feror ego veluti	Hither, thither, masterless
sine nauta navis,	Ship upon the sea,
ut per vias aeris	Wandering through the ways of air,
vaga fertur avis,	Go the birds like me.
non me tenent vincula,	Bound am I by ne'er a bond,
non me tenet clavis,	Prisoner to no key,
quero mei similes,	Questing go I for my kind,
et adiungor pravis. . . .	Find depravity. . . .
Presul discretissime,	Pardon, pray you, good my lord,
veniam te precor:	Master of discretion,
morte bona morior,	But this death I die is sweet,
dulci nece necor,	Most delicious poison.
meum pectus sauciat	Wounded to the quick am I
puellarum decor,	By a young girl's beauty:
et quas tactu nequeo,	She's beyond my touching? Well,
saltem corde mechor. . . .	Can't the mind do duty? . . .
Poculis accenditur	'Tis the fire that's in the cup
animi lucerna,	Kindles the soul's torches,
cor inbutum nectare	'Tis the heart that drenched in wine
volat ad superna;	Flies to heaven's porches.
mihi sapit dulcius	Sweeter tastes the wine to me
vinum de taberna,	In a tavern tankard
quam quod aqua miscuit	Than the watered stuff my Lord
presulis pincerna. . . .	Bishop hath decanted. . . .[42]

Thus the famous *Confession* of the Archpoet, who was a member of the household of Rainald of Dassel, archbishop of Cologne and imperial chancellor in the 1150s and 1160s, and of the small group to whom we owe most of the best of this poetry: Hugh 'Primate', canon of Orleans, and Walter of Châtillon, were the other most notable names. They claimed to live for wine and women, for the tavern rather than the bishop's hall, let alone the Church; to be followers of Golias or Goliath, a symbol of all the vices of the student world. As is common with highly sophisticated literature of this kind –

as with the Provençal lyric and its distant successor, the Shakespearean sonnet – the matter of these poems was no doubt commonly fictitious; some of the poems would lose much of their point if it were not so. What we know of Rainald of Dassel does not suggest that he (or his butler) watered the wine; nor did canons of Orleans lead the Primate's way of life, though some may well have matriculated in the taverns before they passed on to the more dignified houses in the close. But the literary achievement is astonishing. The best of the lyrics have the fresh beauty of the mosaic in the apse of San Clemente; and in them too may be found Cupids and other classical folk playing in a happy and natural setting. The meters and rhythms were not those in which Cupid was born: they have a rapidity, a freedom and a love of rhyme quite alien to the classical lyric poets; but they are a genuine addition to classical Latin literature, in that they reveal a new horizon in the use of Latin, and treat Latin, as most writers of the Middle Ages and the Renaissance could not, as a mother tongue and a medium for original expression.

Clauso Chronos et serato	Time's shut up and Spring
carcere ver exit,	Hath broken prison,
risu Jovis reserato	Into clearer skies
faciem detexit, . . .	Hath the sun arisen,
purpurato	Purple flowers the heath.
floret prato.	Spring, put thy★ kingship on,
ver tenet primatum	Reborn to gleaming beauty
ex algenti	From frozen earth.
renitenti	
specie renatum. . . .	

Vernant veris ad amena	Now springs the thyme in all his
	pleasant places,
–thyma, rose lilia,	Roses and fleur-de-lys,
his alludit filomena,	And Philomel sweet singing
merops et luscinia.	In wanton melody.†

★ Translating *tene*; *tenet* makes 'put his kingship on'.   † Translating *melos et lascivia*.

Conciliaf hostef. tu rumpif federa pacif.

Et qui nulla saunt omnia sare facif.

Vultuf claufa serif tibi pande~ archa thenarif.

Tu daf ut detur. nil dare poffe facif.

Daf ceco uifum. daf claudo crura scelarif.

Crederif effe deuf. hec quia cuncta facif.

Ergo bibamuf ne siramuf. uaf repleamuf.

Quifqui fuof posterior siue prior.

Sic sine cura morte futura repetatur.

Poue metum z talof. pereat qui craftina curet.

Bachuf erat captuf uinculifq; tenacib; aptuf.

Noluit ergo deuf carcerif effe reuf.

Aft inconclauf dirupit uincula suam.

Et factif sonitu pedit clautib;

OTAGORAS. Erquifita licet

sruf siue situ. z bibatuf expediti z cyphor. in obliu cyph

crebro repetiti non dormiant. z sermonef inauditi pro /

sittant. Qui potare non prestif. ite paul ab hif festif. non est hoc

hic modestif. inter letof mof agreftif. modefthe. z e sue certuf testif

132 A drinking song; from the famous manuscript of c. 1225, the *Carmina Burana*, which contains the lyric on pp. 190, 192

Satyro hoc excitat,	The Satyrs are awake,
et Dryadum choreas,	Dancing the Dryads,
redivivis incitatur	The nymphs in the brake
hoc ignibus Napeas.	Kindling for his sake,
	Lit with new fires.
hoc Cupido concitus	O Love,★ by Spring awakened,
hoc amor innovatur,	Desire is born,
hoc ego sollicitus,	And by the spring-fret shaken,
hoc mihi mens furatur.	My mind is torn.
Ignem alo tacitum,	I love, to my undoing,
amo, nec ad placitum,	The flame I tend is hidden,
ut quis contra libitum	And dangerous my wooing,
cupio prohibitum,	Desire of the forbidden.
votis Venus meritum	My goddess in her wisdom
rite facit irritum,	Makes naught of my poor vows,
trudit in interitum	And draws unto his ruin
quem rebar emeritum. . . .	One broken in her wars. . . .[43]

What, in the end, was the movement we call 'the Twelfth Century Renaissance'? It is as if we stood on the slopes above a valley between lofty hills: across the valley is a road running up the further slope and over the hills opposite to us. We cannot see clearly where it comes from, nor the route it takes when it has crossed the hill and gone out of our sight. Such are the movements of history. Yet is is wrong to think the road leads nowhere: it leads to Dante and Petrarch and Chaucer and beyond. Some of the traffic which passed along the road never reached the summit or never passed it; but much went on; and whatever we may now think of the aims and aspirations recorded in this book, the world would have been a poorer place without them.

★ Translating 'o Cupido'.

Map showing places referred to in the text

CHRONOLOGICAL TABLES

This chart lists the authors, major books and works of art discussed, mentioned or illustrated in this book, set against the background of the chief political figures and events of the period. Leading popes, kings and bishops mentioned in the

PAPACY AND EMPIRE: ITALY AND GERMANY		BRITAIN AND FRANCE	
1039–56	Emperor Henry III		
		1042–66	Edward the Confessor
1046	Synod of Sutri: reform of the Papacy		
1049–54	Pope Leo IX		
1056–1106	Emperor Henry IV		
1059–85	Robert Guiscard, first Norman duke of Apulia and Calabria	1060–1108	King Philip I of France
1061	Roger I invades Sicily		
		1066–87	William the Conqueror
1073–85	Pope Gregory VII	1070–89	Lanfranc, archbishop of Canterbury
1075–1122	First contest of Empire and Papacy – 'investiture' disputes		
1077	Henry VI and Gregory VII meet at Canossa		
1088–99	Pope Urban II	1087–1100	William II
1095–99	First Crusade		

text are fitted into columns 1 and 2; but most of the figures and events in these columns are not in fact mentioned elsewhere in the book. Popes, kings and emperors are in italics; in column 2 the English kings are listed by name alone.

AUTHORS, TEACHERS AND BOOKS	CHURCHES AND WORKS OF ART
c. 1000–88 Berengar of Tours	
c. 1033–1109 St Anselm, archbishop of Canterbury	
c. 1040–1116 Ivo, bishop of Chartres	
Late eleventh century *Song of Roland* (earliest surviving form)	
c. 1060–*c.* 1130 Eadmer	
	c. 1070–80 Bayeux Tapestry
c. 1076–1154 Gilbert de la Porrée	
c. 1079–1142 Peter Abelard	
c. 1080–*c.* 1145 William of Conches	1086–1121 Third Church at Cluny ('Cluny III')
1091–1153 St Bernard of Clairvaux	*c.* 1096–1120 Vézelay abbey
	1097–98 Foundation of Cîteaux abbey

PAPACY AND EMPIRE: ITALY AND GERMANY		BRITAIN AND FRANCE	
1099–1118	Pope Paschal II	1100–35	Henry I
1106–25	Emperor Henry V	1108–37	King Louis VI of France
1125–37	Emperor Lothar III	1122–51	Suger, abbot of Saint-Denis
1130–43	Pope Innocent II	1129–71	Henry of Blois, bishop of Winchester
1138–52	Conrad III of Hohenstaufen, King of Germany (never crowned emperor)	1135–54	Stephen
1139–54	Roger the Great, King of Sicily	1137–80	King Louis VII of France
		1139–61	Theobald, archbishop of Canterbury
1147–48	Second Crusade		

AUTHORS, TEACHERS AND BOOKS	CHURCHES AND WORKS OF ART	
Early twelfth century	Theophilus *The Various Arts*	1100–1118	Roger of Helmarshausen, portable altars
		Early twelfth century	San Clemente, Rome
		1107–18	Liège font
fl. 1119–26	Bernard of Chartres	*c.* 1115–30	Moissac abbey, west end (cloister *c.* 1000, later altered)
		c. 1115–33	Durham Cathedral nave
fl. c. 1120–46	Robert Pullen	*c.* 1120	St Albans Psalter
		c. 1120–46	Saint Lazarus, Autun and Gilbert's sculpture (prob. 1125–35)
c. 1125	William of Malmesbury, *History of the Kings of England*	*c.* 1125–30	Old Sarum Cathedral extended (first Norman period 1078–99)
1128–34	Gilbert the Universal, bishop of London		
		c. 1130–40	The Bury Bible
c. 1138	Geoffrey of Monmouth, *History of the Kings of Britain*	1135–44	Saint-Denis, Suger's works
		1135–80	Fountains abbey
c. 1140	Gratian, *Decretum*	1139–47	Fontenay abbey
1141	Completion of Orderic Vitalis, *Ecclesiastical History*	1140–60	Sens Cathedral
c. 1150	Peter the Lombard, *Sentences*	*c.* 1150–55	Chartres, royal portal
		c. 1150–60	Henry of Blois Psalter
		Mid-twelfth century	Martorana and Palatine Chapel, Palermo
		Second half twelfth century	Winchester Bible

PAPACY AND EMPIRE: ITALY AND GERMANY		BRITAIN AND FRANCE	
1152–90	Emperor Frederick I, Barbarossa		
1154–59	Pope Adrian IV	1154–89	Henry II
1159–81	Pope Alexander III	1161–84	Bartholomew, bishop of Exeter
		1162–70	Thomas Becket, archbishop of Canterbury
		1162–81; 1181–83	Peter, formerly abbot of Celle, abbot of Saint Rémi, Rheims, and bishop of Chartres
		1163–87	Gilbert Foliot, bishop of London
1189–98	Third Crusade	1180–1223	Philip II, Augustus, king of France
1190–97	Emperor Henry VI	1189–98	Richard I
1198–1216	Pope Innocent III	1198–1216	John
1204	Fourth Crusade		
1209	Albigensian Crusade		
		1216–72	Henry III
1226	Death of St Francis of Assisi		
1227–41	Pope Gregory IX	1226–70	(St) Louis IX, king of France
1250	Death of Emperor Frederick II		

c. 1155	John of Salisbury, *Entheticus*		
c. 1159	John of Salisbury, *Policraticus* and *Metalogicon*	1160–82	Notre Dame Cathedral, Paris
		1160–1205	Laon Cathedral
1170–90	Chrétien of Troyes' major poems	c. 1172–89	Monreale Cathedral
1173–74	William FitzStephen, *Life of St Thomas Becket* (and description of London)	1174–84 and later	Canterbury Cathedral choir
1181–82	(and later) Walter Map, *De nugis curialium*		
		c. 1190	Lincoln Cathedral choir
		1194–1220	Chartres Cathedral
c. 1200	*Nibelungenlied*		
c. 1200–10	Wolfram von Eschenbach, *Parzival*		
c. 1210–20	Wolfram von Eschenbach, *Willehalm*		
c. 1210	Gottfried von Strassburg, *Tristan*		
1234	*Decretals* of Pope Gregory IX		

NOTES

CHAPTER I

1 Bk ii, *c.* 17; iii, *c.* 5 (ed. A. Griscom, New York, 1929, pp. 273 ff., 282).

2 'The place of England in the twelfth century Renaissance', *History*, XLV (1960), 201–16.

3 Pp. 12–14.

CHAPTER II

4 p. xviii.

5 See Southern, *St. Anselm*, pp. 57 ff.; Brooke, *Europe in the Central Middle Ages*, pp. 316–17.

6 For the later 'school of Chartres' see p. 60.

7 *Making of the Middle Ages*, p. 207.

8 R. W. Southern, *St. Anselm and his Biographer*, p. 101.

9 See the comments of D. Knowles, 'The humanism of the twelfth century', in *The Historian and Character and other essays* (Cambridge 1963), esp. p. 23.

10 See Brooke, *Europe in the Central Middle Ages* (London 1964), pp. 346–7; it is no. 115 in G. Constable's *Letters of Peter the Venerable*, 2 vols. (Cambridge, Mass. 1967) 1, 303–8, esp. pp. 307–8.

CHAPTER III

11 Just possibly Roger the Chancellor: if so, Azo and Roger were the bishop's sons.

12 *Letters*, ed. J. A. Giles (Oxford 1848), no. 167.

13 No. 166.

14 No. 179.

15 Cf. Romans, 13:1.

16 Cf. Ezekiel, *c.* 3.

17 No. 183, cited in A. Morey and Brooke, *Gilbert Foliot and his Letters* (Cambridge 1965), p. 31.

18 The passages cited in the following pages are on pp. 14 ff., 78 ff., 80 ff. of the text and translation by Mrs M. Chibnall (Nelson's Medieval Texts, 1956. The second passage is from Mrs Chibnall's translation, the other two are my own).

CHAPTER IV

19 This is denied in E. Gilson, *Heloise and Abelard*; but see *Cambridge Historical Journal*, XII, i (1956), 4 n.

CHAPTER V

20 And even 'third': see Jurgis Baltrusaitis, *La troisième sculpture Romane* (Formositas Romanica, 1958).

21 See pp. 117, 128.

22 *Antiquaries Journal*, XLVIII (1968), pp. 87–99.

23 Theophilus, *De diversis artibus*, ii, prol., *c.* i; iii, prol., ed. and trans. C. R. Dodwell (Nelson's Medieval Texts, 1961), pp. 36–7, 61–4.

24 What follows is based on D. Grivot and G. Zarnecki, *Gislebertus, Sculptor of Autun* (New York 1961); W. Oakeshott, *Classical Inspiration in Mediaeval Art* (London 1959), chaps. V, VI, esp. pp. 91–2.

25 Now mainly lost, but it has been reconstructed from the surviving fragment and all the available evidence, by Professor K.J. Conant, who has gathered his long study of Cluny into a book, *Cluny* (Macon 1968).

26 *Gislebertus*, p. 13.

27 See J. Bony in *Journal of the Warburg and Courtauld Institutes*, XII (1949), pp. 1–15, esp. pp. 7 ff.

28 *Art. cit.* (n. 22), p. 89.

29 E. Panofsky, *Abbot Suger on the abbey church of Saint-Denis* (Princeton 1946), esp. p. 91 (and, for what follows, pp. 94 ff.).

30 Orderic Vitalis, viii, 26, ed. A. Le Prevost and L. Delisle, III (Paris 1845), p. 445; Walter Map, *De Nugis Curialium*, i, 25, trans. M. R. James (Cymmrodorion Record Series, 1923), p. 49.

31 St Bernard, *Vita Prima*, ii, 5, quoted by Brooke, *Europe in the Central Middle Ages* (London 1964), pp. 70–1. The evidence used in these pages is collected in M. Aubert, *L'architecture cistercienne en France*, I (2nd edn, Paris 1947), esp. pp. 97–8.

32 See F. Bucher in *Comparative Studies in Society and History*, III (1960–1), 89–105; M.-A. Dimier, *Recueil de plans d'églises cisterciennes* (Grignan–Paris 1949).

33 See Brooke, 'Religious sentiment and Church design in the later Middle Ages', *Bulletin of the John Rylands Library*, L (1967), 13–33.

34 F. Wormald, 'The survival of Anglo-Saxon illumination after the Norman Conquest', *Proceedings of the British Academy*, XXX (1944), p. 13. The Weingarten Crucifixion is reproduced *ibid.*; Southern, *Making of the Middle Ages*, frontispiece; Brooke, *From Alfred to Henry III* (Edinburgh 1961), Plate 11.

35 There are still to be seen at Winchester the remains of a draped figure of great beauty which has sometimes been thought to show the influence of Henry's statues. Oakeshott, *Classical Inspiration*, pp. 77–8, suggests that the influence was indirect, via French sculpture, and Professor Zarnecki has pointed out to me its close links with the latest figures on the north transept at Chartres, and suggested a date not earlier than 1220–30. The ultimate classical source is not in doubt. On Henry of Blois as patron, see E. Bishop, *Liturgica Historica*, pp. 392 ff.

36 George Zarnecki, *Later English Romanesque Sculpture*, p. 30.

37 London 1949 (1950), pp. 450–51.

38 *Ibid.*

CHAPTER VI
39 *Gesta Regum* (ed. W. Stubbs, Rolls Series, I, II: cf. for this and what follows, Brooke in *Studies in the Early British Church* (ed. N.K. Chadwick, Cambridge 1958), pp. 231–2.

40 The *Lancelot*, the *Queste*, and the *Mort Artu* form the cycle known as the Prose Lancelot which is the kernel of the 'Vulgate Cycle' of French prose romances; these three were composed *c.* 1215–30, and they are printed in H.O. Sommer's edition of the Cycle (vols. V–VI, 1912–13), and for a convenient summary of recent study, see *Arthurian Literature*, chapter 22 (by J. Frappier). What follows is based on my introduction to the new edition of Walter Map, *De Nugis Curialium*, ed. and trans. M.R. James. The extracts below are in Dist. ii, c. 17; Dist. iv, c. 3; Dist. iii, c. 2 (trans. M.R. James, 1st edn., 1923, pp. 90 ff., esp. 91, 166, 120 ff.).

41 See C.R. Dodwell in *Burlington Magazine*, CVIII (1966), 549–60; and cf. Brooke, *Europe in the Central Middle Ages*, p. 359.

CHAPTER VII
42 From H. Waddell, *Mediaeval Latin Lyrics* (4th edn., London 1933), pp. 170 ff.; the text slightly corrected by F.J.E. Raby, *History of Secular Latin Poetry* (2nd edn., Oxford 1957), II, 183 ff.

43 Waddell, pp. 242–5: the text corrected by the edition of O. Schumann (*Carmina Burana*, ed. A. Hilka and O. Schumann, I, II, Heidelberg 1941, no. 73).

BIBLIOGRAPHICAL NOTES

The major books discussed are C.H. Haskins, *The Renaissance of the*
Twelfth Century (Cambridge, Mass. 1927); G. Paré, A. Brunet, P. Tremblay,
La renaissance du douzième siècle (Paris 1933); E. Panofsky, *Renaissance and
Renascence in Western Art* (Stockholm 1960); R. W. Southern, *The Making
of the Middle Ages* (London 1953). The phrase 'twelfth-century renaissance'
was the subject of a semantic controversy started by W. A. Nitze in
Speculum XXIII (1948), 464–71; *cf.* U.T. Holmes Jr, *ibid.* XXVI (1951),
643–51; *cf.* also, and especially for the contribution of individual countries,
R. W. Southern, 'The place of England in the twelfth century Renaissance',
History XLV (1960), 201–16.

On the themes: schools, scholarship, theology, Anselm, and Abelard, see
the bibliographies in E. Gilson, *History of Christian Philosophy in the Middle
Ages* (London 1955); for short introductions, D. Knowles, *Evolution of
Medieval Thought* (London 1962); A. Forest, F. Van Steenberghen, M. de
Gaudillac, *Le mouvement doctrinal du XIe au XIVe siècle* (Paris 1951 – A.
Fliche and V. Martin (eds.), *Histoire de l'Eglise*, vol. XIII); G. Leff, *Medieval
Thought* (Harmondsworth 1958). J. de Ghellinck, *Le mouvement théologique
du XIIe siècle* (2nd edn., Bruges 1948); M.-D. Chenu, *La théologie du XIIe
siècle* (Paris 1957); B. Smalley, *Study of the Bible in the Middle Ages* (2nd
edn., Oxford 1952); H. Rashdall, *Universities of Europe in the Middle Ages*
(ed. F.M. Powicke and A.B. Emden, 3 vols., Oxford 1936); R. W.
Southern, *St. Anselm and his biographer* (Cambridge 1963); J. G. Sikes,
Peter Abailard (Cambridge 1932); D.E. Luscombe, *The School of Peter
Abelard* (Cambridge 1969); and articles on Abelard and others in *Dictionnaire de théologie catholique* and *Dictionnaire d'histoire et de géographie ecclési-
astiques*; and above all E. Gilson, *Heloise and Abelard* (Eng. trans. London
1953) and Abelard's *Historia calamitatum* and his and Heloise's letters.
The former is ed. J. Monfrin (2nd edn., Paris 1962); both are ed. J.T.
Muckle in *Mediaeval Studies* XII (1950), 163–213 (*Historia*, alias letter 1);
XV (1953), 47–94 (letters 1–4, alias 2–5); XVII (1955), 240–81 (letters 5–6,
alias 6–7); letter 7 (alias 8) is ed. T.P. McLaughlin, *ibid.* XVIII (1956),
241–92; English translations of the *Historia* by Muckle, *The story of
Abelard's adversities* (Toronto 1954); of the *Historia* and letters by C.K.
Scott-Moncrieff (London 1925). For Giraldus Cambrensis, see H. E. Butler,
The Autobiography of Giraldus Cambrensis (London 1937); on German
literature, see below.

JOHN OF SALISBURY
: On humanism, D. Knowles in *The Historian and Character and other essays* (Cambridge 1963), chapter 2; and with particular reference to John of Salisbury, H. Liebeschütz, *Mediaeval Humanism in the Life and Writings of John of Salisbury* (London 1950); *cf.* Liebeschütz's supplementary essay in *Archiv für Kulturgeschichte* L (1968), 1 ff. (in German). On John, see C.C.J. Webb, *John of Salisbury* (London 1932). The quotations are from *Historia Pontificalis*, ed. and trans. M. Chibnall (Nelson's Medieval Texts, 1956: see our Note 18 for translation); *Letters*, ed. and trans. W.J. Millor, H.E. Butler and C.N.L. Brooke, I (Nelson's Medieval Texts, 1955); II, III (Oxford Medieval Texts, forthcoming). The *Policraticus* and *Metalogicon* were ed. C.C.J. Webb (Oxford 1909, 1929); the former translated partly by J. Dickinson (New York 1927), partly by J.B. Pike (Minneapolis 1938); the *Metalogicon* by D. McGarry (Berkeley and Los Angeles 1955); the *Entheticus* was ed. C. Petersen (Hamburg 1843).

MASTER GRATIAN OF BOLOGNA
: On canon law, Z.N. Brooke, *The English Church and the Papacy from the Conquest to the Reign of John* (Cambridge 1931); P. Fournier and G. Le Bras, *Histoire des collections canoniques en Occident* (2 vols., Paris 1931–2); G. Le Bras (ed.), *Histoire du droit et des institutions de l'Église en occident*, esp. vol. VII, *L'Âge classique, 1140–1378* (Paris 1965). On Gratian, see especially S. Kuttner, *Harmony from Dissonance* (Latrobe 1960); the *Decretum* was ed. E. Friedberg (Leipzig 1879). For other individual figures, etc., *Dictionnaire de droit canonique*; for judges delegate, A. Morey, *Bartholomew of Exeter* (Cambridge 1937); for the late twelfth century, C. Duggan, *Twelfth-century Decretal Collections* (London 1963); for Roman Law, P. Vinogradoff, *Roman Law in Medieval Europe* (2nd edn., Oxford 1929). For the papal chancery, R.L. Poole, *Lectures on the History of the Papal Chancery* (Cambridge 1915); C.R. Cheney, *The study of the Medieval Papal Chancery* (Glasgow 1965).

THEOPHILUS, GILBERT AND SUGER
: On art and architecture, the relevant literature is vast, since it includes all good collections of photographs and reproductions. It is particularly true for this period that a week or a month looking at manuscripts or touring Romanesque and early Gothic churches is worth more than many months in a library – so long as our eyes are open, and observant; for this art has to be read like a book. The classic is É. Mâle, *L'Art religieux du XIIe siècle en France* (6th edn., Paris 1953). This chapter is selective, and has been based, in a special measure, on Theophilus, *De diversis artibus*, ed. and trans. C.R. Dodwell (Nelson's Medieval Texts, 1961); D. Grivot and G. Zarnecki, *Gislebertus, Sculptor of Autun* (London 1961); E. Panofsky,

Abbot Suger on the Abbey Church of Saint-Denis (Princeton 1946); O. Pächt, C.R. Dodwell, F. Wormald, *The St Albans Psalter* (London 1960); O. Demus, *The Mosaics of Norman Sicily* (London 1949 (1950)); W. Oakeshott, *Classical Inspiration in Mediaeval Art* (London 1959). On the relations of artists and patrons, see Joan Evans, *Art in Medieval France* (Oxford 1948); on the general setting, G. Duby, *Europe of the Cathedrals* (Geneva 1966); on Romanesque architecture, K.J. Conant, *Carolingian and Romanesque Architecture* (Harmondsworth 1959) and the books of A.W. Clapham on continental and English Romanesque architecture; on painting, A. Grabar and C. Nordenfalk, *Romanesque Painting* (Geneva 1958); J. Ainaud and A. Held, *Romanesque Painting* (Contact History of Art, 1963); on sculpture, the books of G. Zarnecki, especially *English Romanesque Sculpture, 1066–1140* and *Later English Romanesque Sculpture* (London 1951, 1953). On Anglo-Saxon art, F. Wormald, *English Drawings of the tenth and eleventh centuries* (London 1952); and for the consequences of the Norman Conquest, Wormald's article cited in our Note 34; C.R. Dodwell, *The Canterbury School of Illumination* (Cambridge 1954); for a general survey, T.S.R. Boase, *English Art, 1100–1216* (Oxford History of Art, III, 1953), with useful bibliography. On Cistercian architecture, see M. Aubert, *L'architecture cistercienne en France* (2nd edn., 2 vols., Paris 1947), and see our Note 32. On Cluniac, J. Evans, *Romanesque Architecture of the Order of Cluny* and *Cluniac Art of the Romanesque Period* (Cambridge 1938, 1949). On liturgy and religious sentiment, E. Bishop, *Liturgica Historica* (Oxford 1918; and on Henry of Blois as patron, pp. 392 ff.); D. Knowles, *Monastic Order in England* (Cambridge 1940; 2nd edn. 1963); A. Wilmart, *Auteurs spirituels et textes dévots du moyen âge latin* (Paris 1932); and the articles by Bucher and Brooke cited in our Notes 32 and 33. On Gothic origins, Panofsky, *Abbot Suger* (above); O. von Simson, *The Gothic Cathedral* (New York 1956); J. Harvey, in the *Antiquaries Journal* XLVIII (1968), 87–99; and for a general survey, P. Frankl, *Gothic Architecture* (Harmondsworth 1962).

For convenience, one may divide the material into two parts: history and pseudo-history, and vernacular literature. On history and biography, and especially on Eadmer, see R.W. Southern, *St. Anselm and his biographer* (Cambridge 1963); Eadmer's *Vita Anselmi*, ed. and trans. R.W. Southern (Nelson's Medieval Texts, 1962); *Historia Novorum*, ed. M. Rule (Rolls Series, 1884), trans. G. Bosanquet (London 1964). On William of Malmesbury, introduction to *Gesta Regum*, ed. W. Stubbs (2 vols., Rolls Series, 1887–9); trans. J.A. Giles (London 1847); *Historia Novella*, ed. and trans.

K. Potter (Nelson's Medieval Texts, 1955); *Vita Wulfstani*, ed. R.R. Darlington (Camden Third Series, XL, London 1928), trans. J.H.F. Peile (Oxford 1934); on his research techniques, see J. Armitage Robinson, *Somerset Historical Essays* (London 1921), chapters 1, 2; and, in a wider context, the penetrating study by V.H. Galbraith, *Historical Research in Medieval England* (London 1951). There is a general account of 'William of Malmesbury's Life and Works' by H. Farmer in *Journal of Ecclesiastical History* XIII (1962), 39–54 (see also *idem*, in *Latin Biography*, ed. T.A. Dorey, London 1967, chapter VII). On Orderic see Mrs M. Chibnall's introduction to her new edition and translation, vol. II (Oxford Medieval Texts, 1968), and Delisle's to the old edition by A. Le Prevost and L. Delisle (Paris 1838–55), vol. v. Geoffrey of Monmouth's *Historia Regum Britanniae* has been many times edited (recently by A. Griscom, New York 1929, and E. Faral, *La légende arthurienne*, I, iii, Paris 1929)★ and many times translated (e.g. in the Bohn, Everyman and Penguin series). The fullest commentary is J.S.P. Tatlock, *The Legendary History of Britain* (Berkeley, California 1950).

Geoffrey and the Arthurian literature – including *Parzival* and *Tristan* – are embraced in the encyclopedic *Arthurian Literature in the Middle Ages*, ed. R.S. Loomis (Oxford 1959) – of unequal critical merit, but a mine of information; *cf.* also W.T.H. Jackson, *The Literature of the Middle Ages* (New York 1960). On the German literature, see the short introduction by P.B. Salmon, *Literature in medieval Germany* (London 1967; with appendix of further reading); on a larger scale, H. de Boor and R. Newald, *Geschichte der deutschen Literatur*, vols. I, II (Munich 1949–53); and the classic by Julius Schwittering, *Die deutsche Dichtung des Mittelalters* (Potsdam 1932 ff.). On Wolfram von Eschenbach, see especially H. Sacker, *An Introduction to Wolfram's Parzival* (Cambridge 1963).† Editions and translations are listed in Sacker, *Introduction*, p. 196; helpful to the newcomer is M.F. Richey, *Studies of Wolfram von Eschenbach* (Edinburgh 1957). The *Nibelungenlied* and *Tristan* have both been translated by A.T. Hatto

---

★ A variant version was ed. J. Hammer (Medieval Academy of America, 1951): its relation to the normal text is still *sub judice*. If the view held by some scholars, that it is earlier than the vulgate text, proved correct, some revision of detail, though not of the substance, of what is said on pp. 166–67 would be necessary.

† I owe my introduction to Wolfram to Mr Sacker, on whose unpublished 'The Tolerance Idea in Wolfram's *Willehalm*' (Doctoral Thesis, Frankfurt-am-Main 1955), my account of Willehalm is based (see also p. 155 ff.).

The section on Wolfram in general is based on some paragraphs in my chapter in *The Layman in Christian History*, ed. S.C. Neill and H.-R. Weber (London 1963), pp. 123–6, from which a few sentences and expressions have been repeated (with the permission of the World Council of Churches).

in Penguin Classics (1965, 1960), with bibliography. See also G. Weber, *Gottfried von Strassburg* (in German: in the useful series, *Sammlung Metzler*, Stuttgart 1962). Of the Chansons de Geste, *The Song of Roland* is available in many versions, including the Penguin Classic by Dorothy Sayers. The view that it was a work of original literature, not a traditional oral poem, was brilliantly expounded by J. Bédier in *Les légendes épiques* (4 vols., Paris 1908–13); this was effectively countered by R. Menéndez Pidal, *La chanson de Roland et la tradition épique des Francs* (Paris 1960) – although disputes about these poems will continue till the end of time. On their relation to the Bayeux Tapestry, see C. R. Dodwell in *Burlington Magazine* CVIII (1966), 549–60; on the Tapestry itself, the Phaidon Press edition has the fullest commentary (ed. Sir F. Stenton, 2nd edn., 1965). On Chrétien, see the general introduction by J. Frappier in *Arthurian Literature*, chapter 15, with notes on literature and editions; all his major works except *Perceval* are available in W. W. Comfort's prose translation in the Everyman Library; *Perceval* was translated by R. W. Linker (Chapel Hill 1952). On the French literature two classics, both now dated but well worth reading still, are W. P. Ker, *Epic and Romance* (London 1896) and C. S. Lewis, *The Allegory of Love* (Oxford 1936), chapter 1.

Two themes are treated, only summarily referred to earlier in the book. The first is translations from Greek and Arabic, on which see C. H. Haskins, *Studies in the History of Medieval Science* (Cambridge, Mass. 1924), and the various works of A. C. Crombie, summarized in his chapter in *Medieval England*, ed. A. L. Poole (Oxford 1958), II, 571–604. On Latin literature in general, J. de Ghellinck, *L'essor de la littérature latine au XIIᵉ siècle* (Brussels–Paris 1946); on Latin poetry, F. J. E. Raby, *History of Christian-Latin Poetry* (2nd edn., Oxford 1953) and *History of Secular Latin Poetry in the Middle Ages* (2nd edn., 2 vols., Oxford 1957) – which contains the best study of the medieval Latin Lyric, whose inspiration has been revealed to recent generations by Helen Waddell's *Medieval Latin Lyrics* (here quoted from 4th edn., London 1933; many times reprinted) and *The Wandering Scholars* (London 1927). For the new edition of the *Carmina Burana*, see our Note 43.

THIS BOOK will have served a purpose if a few readers are induced to read widely in the sources and literature of the twelfth century; and for English readers a useful guide is C. P. Farrar and A. P. Evans, *Bibliography of English Translations from Medieval Sources* (Columbia Records of Civilization, New York 1946). It will have answered its author's prayer if a few are induced to search for the twelfth century with knapsack and binoculars.

LIST OF ILLUSTRATIONS

1 Arthur before Geoffrey of Monmouth. Modena Cathedral, Italy: detail of doorway, probably 1099–1120 (see *Arthurian Literature of the Middle Ages*, ed. R.S. Loomis, Oxford, 1959, pp. 60–2; E. *Mâle, L'art religieux du XIIe siècle*, 4th ed., Paris 1940, pp. 267ff. – Mâle dated it later in the century). Photo: U. Orlandini, Modena

2 Constantine the Great at Parthenay-le-Vieux: tympanum of the church of St Hilaire, twelfth century. (For plates 2–5 see J. Adhémar, *Influences antiques dans l'art du moyen âge français, Studies of the Warburg Institute*, VII (1939), 208ff.; G. Zarnecki, *Later English Romanesque Sculpture*, London 1953, pp. 12ff.; Mâle, pp. 247ff.; R. Crozet in *Cahiers de Civilisation Médiévale*, I (1958), 27ff.). Photo: Archives Photographiques, Paris

3 Constantine at Poitiers: eleventh–twelfth century wall-painting in the Baptistery. Photo: Hirmer Fotoarchiv, Munich

4 Marcus Aurelius, bronze equestrian statue, Rome, Capitol – believed in the Middle Ages to be a statue of Constantine. Photo: Mansell Collection

5 St George and the Dragon; tympanum of the church of St George, Brinsop (Herefordshire), twelfth century. Photo: National Monuments Record

6 Boethius sitting with his tablets in the initial of the first book of his *Consolations of Philosophy*: Oxford, Bodleian Library, MS Auct. F. 6.5, f. vii v (twelfth century). Photo: Bodleian Library

7 Aristotle, from the west front of Chartres cathedral, mid-twelfth century. He sits at the feet of Dialectic in a group of the seven liberal arts on the arch of the right-hand tympanum on the west front. Photo: Bildarchiv Foto Marburg

8, 9, 10 The Professions, from the Reuner Musterbuch, c. 1208–18, Vienna, Nationalbibliothek, MS 507, ff. 2 r–v. (See H.J. Hermann, *Die Deutschen Romanischen Handschriften*, Leipzig 1926 –, *Beschreibendes Verzeichnis der illuminierten HSS in Österreich*, VIII, ii, pp. 353–8). Weavers at work (8); a farmer, perhaps a village reeve, supervises his ploughmen (9); a scribe and a painter (10). Photo: Österreichische Nationalbibliothek, Vienna

11 The orders of society. A knight presents land to the Dean of Sainte-Croix-d'Orléans, for his dependent church of St Georges, Mervilliers. A mould at Chartres Museum from the tympanum formerly at Mervilliers. Photo: Chartres Museum

12 The library in the St Gallen monastic plan: this famous ninth century plan of an imaginary monastery is preserved in the Stiftsbibliothek at St Gallen (cf. H. Reinhart, *Der St Gallerr Klosterplan*, St Gallen 1952). Photo: Stiftsbibliothek St Gallen

13 A twelfth century wooden book cupboard, now in the Musée de Valère, Sion (Valais, Switzerland). Photo: Musée de Valère

14 A twelfth century book cupboard, let into the cloister wall in the Augustinian abbey of Lilleshall (Shropshire). Photo: C.N.L. Brooke

15 Fulbert, bishop of Chartres, in his cathedral; from the memorial volume made immediately after his death in 1028, formerly in Chartres cathedral, destroyed in the Second World War. From R. Merlet and A. Clerval, *Un manuscrit chartrain du XIe siècle*, (Chartres 1893), facing p. 227. Photo: J.R. Freeman

16 Lanfranc, prior of Bec, abbot of Caen, Archbishop of Canterbury (1070–89), from a twelfth century manuscript of his *Liber de Corpore et Sanguine Domini* against Berengar: Oxford, Bodleian Library, MS Bodl. 569, f. 1. Photo: Bodleian Library

17 Hugh of St Victor (*fl. c.* 1125–41), head of the school of St-Victor, Paris, mother house of the Victorine congregation of Augustinian canons. From an early thirteenth century manuscript of his *De arca morali* formerly in the library of St Albans abbey, now Oxford, Bodleian Library, MS Laud Misc. 409 (f. 3v). Photo: Bodleian Library

18 Palermo, a panorama of the city, from Bern, Burgerbibliothek, MS 120/II, f.98 – Petrus de Ebulo, *Liber ad Honorem Augusti*, 1195–6. See *Schätze der Burgerbibliothek, Bern*, Bern 1953, pp. 120–3. Photo: Bern, Burgerbibliothek

19 Palermo, the royal court, from the same MS, f. 101. Photo: Bern, Burgerbibliothek

20 From a thirteenth century MS of Euclid: Oxford, Bodleian Library, MS Auct. F.5.28, f. 101v. Photo: Bodleian Library

21 Surgery: treatment of the eyes and nose, from a twelfth century Herbal of Dioscorides: British Museum, Harleian MS 1585, f.9v. Photo: British Museum

22 A peacock, from a twelfth century Bestiary: Oxford, Bodleian Library, Ashmole MS 1511, f. 72r. Photo: Bodleian Library

23 Blackberries, from an early twelfth century Herbal: Oxford, Bodleian Library, MS Bodl. 130, f. 26r. Photo: Bodleian Library

24 The Glossa Ordinaria. A portion of Leviticus (16:20), from a twelfth century glossed Bible. See B. Smalley, *The Study of the Bible in the Middle Ages* (2nd ed., Oxford 1952). From a MS of 1176 (from the Cistercian abbey of Buildwas, Shropshire). British Museum, Harleian MS. 3038 f. 39. Photo: British Museum

25 Christ the Ruler. A twelfth century Limoges enamel book cover, in the Louvre. Photo: Service de Documentation Photographique, Réunion des Musées Nationaux

26 Satan as a fallen angel. From the Munich Gospels of the Emperor Otto III, c. 1000 (see E. Mâle, L'art religieux du XIIe siècle, p. 370; C.R. Dodwell and D.H. Turner, Reichenau revisited, London 1965, p. 28). Munich, Bayerische Staatsbibliothek, MS 4453, f.32 v. Photo: Bayerische Staatsbibliothek, Munich

27 The Demonic Satan from the mouth of Hell in the Henry of Blois Psalter, c. 1150–60: British Museum, Cotton MS Nero C. iv, f.39. Photo: British Museum

28 Gilbert's Satan, tempting Christ, nave capital in Autun cathedral, early twelfth century (see D. Grivot and G. Zarnecki, Gislebertus, Sculptor of Autun, New York 1961, p.73). Photo: Jean Roubier

29 The comic devil from the Bohemian Codex Gigas (1204–30). Stockholm, Royal Library, MS Halm A.148, f.290r. Photo: Royal Library, Stockholm

30 The deposition from the Cross, from an ivory, probably Spanish, of the eleventh or twelfth century, in the Victoria and Albert Museum. Photo: Victoria and Albert Museum

31 Jesus, both crowned and suffering, from a wooden cross in the Museo at Vich (Barcelona), twelfth or thirteenth century. Photo: MAS Barcelona

32 Jesus as a pilgrim, from a French manuscript of the twelfth century: Cambrai, Bibl. de Ville, MS 528, f.1. Photo: Bibliothèque Nationale, Paris

33 Jesus as a knight, from the reliquary of St Hadelin, in the church of Vise (Belgium), eleventh century. Photo: ACL, Brussels

34 Map of the world, with Jerusalem in the centre, from a thirteenth century English Psalter: British Museum, Addit. MS 28,681, f.9. Photo: British Museum

35 The Church of the Holy Sepulchre, Jerusalem. Plan in an early thirteenth century copy of Adamnan, De locis sanctis, written at Reun (Cistercian abbey): Österreichische Nationalbibliothek, MS 609, f.4 (see Hermann, pp. 362–4). Photo: Österreichische Nationalbibliothek

36 Old Sarum from the air: the site of John of Salisbury's birth-place, with the Norman castle and cathedral set in ancient ramparts (see M.W. Beresford and J.K.S. St Joseph, Medieval England: an aerial survey, Cambridge 1958, pp. 185–7). Photo: J.K.S. St Joseph, copyright of Cambridge University Committee for Aerial Photography

37 The great seal of Henry II; the 'first seal': British Museum, Doubleday Cast, A28 (W. de G. Birch, Catalogue of Seals in the British Museum, I, London 1887, p. 10; cf. A.B. Wyon, Great Seals of England, London 1887, p. 15 and pl. V, nos. 30–1). The cast was taken from Public Record Office, D.L. 10/23, on which see T.A.M. Bishop, Scriptores Regis, Oxford 1961, p. 57, no. 424. Photo: British Museum

38 Signatures of pope and cardinals to a solemn bull or privilege of Pope Adrian IV. These were partly written by their clerks, partly by themselves (British Museum, Addit. Charter 66,715; on signatures to bulls, see B. Katterbach and W.M. Peitz, in Miscellanea Francesco Ehrle, IV, Rome 1924, pp. 177–274). Photo: British Museum

39 John of Salisbury's Entheticus: a page from the only early MS: British Museum, Royal 13. D. iv, f.213v. This MS was presented to St Albans abbey by Abbot Simon (1167–83) and was therefore probably written in John's lifetime. Photo: British Museum

40 Man as the microcosm: a twelfth century picture showing man as the microcosm of the four elements of which the world is composed, surrounded by the four winds. From a German astronomical manuscript written at Prüfening, Bavaria, end of twelfth century. Vienna, Österreichische Nationalbibliothek, MS 12,600, f.29r. Photo: Österreichische Nationalbibliothek

41 Twelfth century chasuble, traditionally supposed to be Thomas Becket's. Sens, Cathédrale, Trésor. Photo: Giraudon

42 Henry II's tomb at Fontevrault. Photo: Giraudon

43 Becket's murder, from British Museum, Cotton MS Claudius B.ii, f.341r, late twelfth century: a fair copy, perhaps executed at Canterbury under the editor's eye, of Alan of Tewkesbury's edition of the correspondence of the Becket dispute. This picture is set at the head of John of Salisbury's letter giving the earliest account of the murder, and the picture may be the earliest surviving of the event (on the others see T. Borenius, St Thomas Becket in Art, London 1932, and addenda in Archaeologia, LXXXI (1931), 19 ff.; LXXXIII (1933), 171 ff. – Borenius did not refer to this MS).[*] Photo: British Museum

44 'Cristus Vincit Cristus Reinat', on a sword made for Henry II's grandson, the Emperor Otto IV, c. 1200; at the Schatzkammer, Vienna. Photo: Kunsthistorisches Museum

45 A twelfth century gold ring set with late antique gem engraved with the figure of Minerva. Legend around the bezel reads: ɪ + S(IGILLUM) RICHARD(I) REG(IS) P(RIVATUM). Probably the personal signet ring of Richard I (1189–99). Photo: British Museum

46 Ivo of Chartres: a twelfth century copy of his Panormia: Jesus College, Oxford, MS 50, f.2r (on the Panormia see Z.N. Brooke, The English Church and the Papacy, Cambridge 1931, esp. pp. 94 ff., 244–5). Photo: Bodleian Library

---

[*] My attention was first drawn to this picture by Professor Sir Roger Mynors.

47 The law of marriage, from a twelfth century copy of Gratian: Corpus Christi College, Cambridge, MS 10, f.268 – to Causa 27, on marriage and religious vows. By courtesy of the Master and Fellows of Corpus Christi College, Cambridge. Photo: Courtauld Institute

48 Papal judges delegate. Seven bishops, acting as delegates of Pope Adrian IV, settle a case between Theobald, archbishop of Canterbury, and the abbot of St Augustine's abbey, Canterbury, 17 July 1157 (Canterbury Cathedral Chartae Antiquae, A51; for the text, see *Acta of the Bishops of Chichester, 1075–1207*, ed. H. Mayr-Harting, Canterbury and York Society, 1964, no. 21; *Letters and Charters of Gilbert Foliot*, ed. A. Morey and C.N.L. Brooke, Cambridge, 1967, no. 293). By courtesy of the Dean and Chapter of Canterbury Cathedral. Photo: Entwistle Photographic Service, Canterbury

49 Marriage as the key to the passage of landed property. From a manuscript compiled at the order of Alfonso II of Aragon (1162–96): the *Liber Feudorum Major* (Barcelona, Archivo de la Corona de Aragón). Photo: MAS, Barcelona

50 Jesus at the marriage at Cana in Galilee, from a twelfth century Austrian manuscript: Vienna, Österreichische Nationalbibliothek, MS 2739, f.41r. See Hermann, pp. 249–58. Photo: Österreichische Nationalbibliothek

51 Family life in the Reuner Musterbuch (see our p. 26; ills. 8–10). Ibid., MS 507, f. iv. Photo: Österreichische Nationalbibliothek

52 The marriage of Christ and the Church, from a twelfth century copy of Bede's Commentary on the Song of Songs: King's College, Cambridge, MS 19, f.21v. Photo: Edward Leigh, Cambridge, by courtesy of the Provost and Fellows of King's College

53 Autun, Porte d'Arroux (Roman gateway). Photo: Jean Roubier

54 Autun cathedral, nave arcade (partly based on Porte d'Arroux). Photo: Jean Roubier

55 Durham cathedral, nave arcade and vault, of the 1120s. Photo: Hürlimann

56 Saint-Denis, Suger's ambulatory (see our pp. 129–32). See E. Panofsky, *Abbot Suger on the abbey church of Saint-Denis*, Princeton 1946. Photo: Hürlimann

57 German Romanesque: the east end of Speyer cathedral, eleventh–twelfth centuries. Photo: Bildarchiv Foto Marburg

58 Vézelay abbey in Burgundy: the tympanum above the west door with the vista of the church opening below. Photo: Jean Roubier

59 February in the calendar in the *St Albans Psalter* (p. 4; ed. O. Pächt, C.R. Dodwell, F. Wormald, London 1960, pl. 3). Photo: Warburg Institute

60 Gilbert's February on the west door of Autun cathedral (Grivot and Zarnecki, *Gislebertus*, pp. 28–9, and pl. 07). Photo by courtesy of the Trianon Press

61 February in the calendar on the west front of Amiens cathedral, c. 1230. Photo: Bildarchiv Foto Marburg

62 Bronze font at Liège, 1107–18, showing the baptism of Jesus resting on twelve oxen. Cf. the interpretation by Rupert of Deutz of II Chronicles, cited by W. Oakeshott in *Classical Inspiration in Mediaeval Art*, London 1959, pp. 87ff. Photo: ACL, Brussels

63 Building in the twelfth century. Palermo, Palatine Chapel, mosaic: masons at work on the Tower of Babel, mid-twelfth century (see O. Demus, *The Mosaics of Norman Sicily*, London 1949–50, esp. pl. 32B). Photo: Scala

64 Moslem influence on Gothic architecture. The arcade of the Great Mosque at Diyarbakir in south-east Turkey, 1117–25 (see John Harvey in *Antiquaries Journal*, XLVIII (1968), 87–99, esp. pl. XXXIIIa). Photo: J. Harvey

65 The presentation of churches by their patrons. The presentation of the church of Avenas by King Louis, perhaps Louis VI (1108–37), to St Vincent. Photo: Bildarchiv Foto Marburg

66 The presentation of Autun cathedral, perhaps by Hugh II, duke of Burgundy, to Étienne de Bagé, bishop of Autun, by the sculptor Gilbert (for this and previous ill. see Grivot and Zarnecki, *Gislebertus*, pp. 67–8 and pls. 13, B9–10). Photo: Jean Roubier

67 The presentation of Monreale cathedral by King William II of Sicily (1166–89) to the Blessed Virgin (O. Demus, pl. 76B). Photo: Scala

68 St Dunstan at Christ's feet, from a contemporary drawing (tenth century) ascribed to Dunstan himself: Oxford, Bodleian Library, MS Auct. F. 4. 32, f. 1 (see F. Wormald, *English Drawings of the Tenth and Eleventh Centuries*, London 1952, pp. 23–5 and pl. 1). Photo: Bodleian Library

69 Extract from a document purporting to be of 1100, referring to the *scrinium* of the monk Roger (our ill. 70). The reference doubtless comes from an authentic source, though the document itself has been supposed a thirteenth century forgery: see K. Honselmann, *Von der Carta zur Siegelkunde*, Paderborn 1939, pp. 1939, pp. 155ff.,* whose arguments however, do not altogether carry conviction. Paderborn, Archiv des Erzbischöfl. Vikariats, Gen. vik. no. 11. Photo: Rolf Ertmer, Paderborn

---

* I owe this reference to the kindness of the staff of the Archiv des Erzbischöfl. Generalvikariats, Paderborn.

70 Roger of Helmarshausen's portable altar or reliquary (or coffer – 'scrinium'), of 1100 (see above). See A. Fuchs, *Die Tragaltäre des Rogerus in Paderborn*, Paderborn 1916; C.R. Dodwell's edn. of Theophilus, *De diversis artibus* (Nelson's Medieval Texts, 1961), pp. xli ff. Photo: Bildarchiv Foto Marburg

71 Chartres cathedral, Charlemagne window, detail: c. 1210–20

72 A Cistercian monk cutting timber (the brown habit occurs in the earliest illuminated MSS from Cîteaux). From the Bibliothèque de Dijon, MS 173, f. 41r (1111). Photo: R. Remy, Dijon

73 Theophilus, *De diversis artibus*, bk. iii, prologue, in MS Wolfenbüttel, Herzog-August Bibliothek MS Guelph Gudianus, lat. 2° 69, f. 98, first half of the twelfth century. On the MS see C.R. Dodwell's edn., pp. lvii ff. Photo: Herzog-August Bibliothek, Wolfenbüttel

74 Solomon's Temple, a plan from a German MS, early twelfth century: Österreichische Nationalbibliothek MS 10, f. 325r. On the MS, see Hermann, *op. cit.*, pp. 50–1. Photo: Österreichische Nationalbibliothek

75, 76 The joys of heaven and the rewards of eternal life: details from the Last Judgment, mosaic in Torcello cathedral (see *Flowering of the Middle Ages*, ed. J. Evans, London 1966, pp. 232–3). Photo: Scala

77 A cover for a Gospel Book, from the Sion Gospels (cf. our ill. 13), c. 1000, with a twelfth century central panel: Victoria and Albert Museum. Photo: Victoria and Albert Museum

78 A small German reliquary from Bamberg, tenth to thirteenth century setting of late classical onyx: Stockholm, Statens Historiska Museum. Photo: Antikvarisk-Topografiska Arkivei

79 A twelfth century German reliquary, the Eltenberg Reliquary from Cologne, now in the Victoria and Albert Museum. Photo: Victoria and Albert Museum

80 Bust-reliquary of St Baudime from Saint-Nectaire, France, end of twelfth century (see J. Taralon, *Treasures of the Churches of France*, London 1966, pp. 262–3)

81 A twelfth century chalice from Rheims, now in Toledo cathedral Treasury. Photo: MAS Barcelona

82 Jesus as a boy, in royal robes, thirteenth century, from Toledo cathedral Treasury (Spanish). Photo: MAS, Barcelona

83 Cluny, capital from ambulatory: Fourth Tone of Music, early twelfth century (model for 84: see J. Evans, *Cluniac Art of the Romanesque Period*, Cambridge 1950, pp. 116f.; Grivot and Zarnecki, *Gislebertus*, p. 74 and pls. B17–18). Photo: Bildarchiv Foto Marburg

84 Autun cathedral, nave capital: Fourth Tone of Music by Gilbert (Grivot and Zarnecki, p. 74 and pls. 34, B17–18). Photo: Jean Roubier

85 'GISLEBERTUS HOC FECIT' – 'This is Gilbert's work': the sculptor's signature at Christ's feet in the Last Judgment over the west door, Autun cathedral (see Grivot and Zarnecki, *Gislebertus*, pp. 13, 25ff.). Photo: Jean Roubier

86 Detail from the Last Judgment, Autun cathedral (see our ill. 85; Grivot and Zarnecki, *Gislebertus*, p. 27): archangel and devil weighing souls. Photo: Jean Roubier

87 Gilbert's *Eve*, Autun, Musée Rolin, formerly in the cathedral, on the lintel of the north transept doorway (see Grivot and Zarnecki, pp. 149ff. and pl. I). Photo: Jean Roubier

88 Gallo-Roman relief of a reclining figure, from Beaune, Musée des Beaux Arts. Photo: Musée des Beaux Arts, Beaune

89 Signature of Girauldus on the tympanum at Saint-Ursin, Bourges, twelfth century. Photo: Jean Roubier

90 'W. de Brail' me fecit': signature of painter portrayed as escaping the Last Judgment, from a MS of c. 1240: Cambridge, Fitzwilliam Museum, MS 330. Photo: Fitzwilliam Museum

91 Hugo Pictor: signature of the Anglo-Norman painter Hugh in a MS of c. 1100: Oxford, Bodleian Library, MS Bodl. 717, f. 287v. Photo: Bodleian Library

92 The sculptor on the bronze doors of S. Zeno Maggiore, Verona, twelfth century. Photo: Alinari/Mansell

93 Canterbury cathedral priory, plan of the precinct and its waterworks, from the Eadwine Psalter, mid twelfth century: Cambridge, Trinity College MS R.17.1, ff. 284v–5. See *The Canterbury Psalter*, ed. M.R. James, London 1935, pp. 53ff.; W. Urry, *Canterbury under the Angevin Kings*, London 1967, pp. 3–4, 204. Photo: By permission of the Master and Fellows of Trinity College, Cambridge

94 Canterbury cathedral choir (see our pp. 124ff; J. Bony, in *Journal of the Warburg and Courtauld Institutes*, XII (1949), 1–15, esp. pp. 7ff.). Photo: Hürlimann

95 Sens cathedral. Photo: Hürlimann

96 Abbot Suger (see our ill. 56) as donor, in Saint-Denis, window. Photo: Archives Photographiques, Paris

97 Suger's eagle vase, an antique Egyptian porphyry, adapted by Suger for use in Saint-Denis. Paris, Louvre. Photo: Giraudon

98 Suger's sardonyx chalice, of gold and precious stones, c. 1140, partly Greco-Roman. Washington, National Gallery. Photo: Washington, National Gallery

99 A group of Suger's columns on the west door of Saint-Denis. Photo: Archives Photographiques, Paris

100 The base from a cross formerly in the abbey of Saint-Bertin, Saint-Omer, now in Saint-Omer, Musée; an imitation of Abbot Suger's great cross, now lost. See Mâle, pp. 153 ff.; Panofsky, *Abbot Suger*, pp. 177 f. Photo: Giraudon

101 The handwriting of Orderic Vitalis: Paris, Bibliothèque Nationale, MS Lat. 5506.2, f. 199v (written in 1141: see edn. of A. Le Prevost and L. Delisle, Paris 1838–55, III, 135; V, pp. xlvff.; cf. edn. of M. Chibnall II (Oxford Medieval Texts, 1968), pp. xxxixff.). Photo: Bibliothèque Nationale

102 Fountains abbey: the west front of the church and the west range, with lay brothers' refectory, etc., below and dormitory above. Photo: Jean Roubier

103 Fontenay abbey church, looking east. Photo: Archives Photographiques, Paris

104 St Ethelwold blessing, with a bare altar and low screens: Benedictional of St Ethelwold, British Museum Addit. MS 49, 598, f. 118v (cf. F. Wormald, *The Benedictional of St Ethelwold*, London 1959, pl. 8). Photo: British Museum

105 San Clemente, Rome, choir looking east (see Brooke in *Bulletin of John Rylands Library*, L (1967), 17–18; for the date of San Clemente, L. Boyle, in *Archivum Fratrum Praedicatorum*, XXX (1960), 417–27). Photo: Alinari/Mansell

106 Two candles on the altar, from the Bohemian Coronation Gospels of c. 1085: Prague, University Library, MS xiv. A.13, f. 20v. Photo: Foto Státni i Knihovna ČSSR, Prague

107 Candles on the altar, from a late twelfth century miniature of the consecration of Cluny abbey in 1095: Paris, Bibliothèque Nationale, MS, Lat. 17, 716, f. 91r (cf. *Flowering of the Middle Ages*, pp. 46–7). Photo: Bibliothèque Nationale

108 The Gloucester candlestick, detail (see E.H. Gombrich, *The Story of Art*, 11th edn., London 1966, p. 125), early twelfth century. Victoria and Albert Museum. Photo: Victoria and Albert Museum

109 The Visitation from the St Albans Psalter (see the edn. of O. Pächt, C.R. Dodwell, F. Wormald, London 1960). Photo: Warburg Institute

110 Eastern influence illustrated by a portable reliquary traditionally associated with St Petroc's relics, now in St Petroc's parish church, Bodmin: twelfth century. For the story of the relics, see G.H. Doble, in *Antiquity* XIII (1939), 403–15. By courtesy of the Borough of Bodmin and the Vicar of Bodmin.* Photo: Clifford R. Clemens, Bodmin

111 Henry of Blois' plaques, British Museum, mid-twelfth century. Photo: British Museum

112 Wolvesey castle, Winchester, from the air. The main structure of the castle was built by Henry of Blois, though there are many later additions and changes, and the present house is of the seventeenth century. Photo: Aerofilms Ltd.

113 Classical influence in twelfth century Winchester: capital of a centaur from the cathedral, late twelfth century. Photo: National Monuments Record

114 Winchester cathedral, twelfth century font of Tournai marble, detail: three men in a boat, from a miracle of St Nicholas. Photo: Jean Roubier

115 St Paul shakes the viper off his hand at Melita (Malta), wall-painting in St Anselm's chapel, Canterbury cathedral, late twelfth century. See E.W. Tristram, *English Medieval Wall-painting: the twelfth century* (Oxford 1944), pp. 21–4. Photo: Hirmer

116 St Paul after his conversion: mosaic in the Palatine chapel, Palermo, mid-twelfth century. See O. Demus, *The Mosaics of Norman Sicily*, p. 450. Photo: Scala

117 The death of the Virgin in the Henry of Blois Psalter, c. 1150–60: British Museum, Cotton MS Nero C. iv, f. 29. See our p. 149. Photo: British Museum

118 The death of the Virgin in the Chiesa della Martorana, Palermo, twelfth century. Photo: Scala

119 Wolfram von Eschenbach, from the famous Minnesinger MS of c. 1315: Heidelberg, Manessischen Liederhandschrift MS Pal. germ. 848, f. 149v. Photo: Universitäts-bibliothek, Heidelberg

120 The Song of Roland. Fighting scene illustrating twelfth century MS of Song of Roland: British Museum, MS Lansdowne 782, f. 27. Photo: British Museum

121 Spanish relief of Roland, second half of twelfth century, from Estella, Navarre. Photo: MAS, Barcelona

122 St James, as slayer of the Moors, from the tympanum, cathedral of Santiago (St James) de Compostela, second half of the twelfth century. Photo: MAS, Barcelona

---

* For my knowledge of the reliquary, and for help in obtaining a photograph, I am very much indebted to the Reverend Canon G.W.S. Harmer, Vicar of Bodmin.

123 Baptism and conversion. St Peter, baptizing, and a monk being slain, from Roger's altar (see our p. 107). Photo: Bildarchiv Foto Marburg

124 The conversion of a Jewish boy; thirteenth century stained glass window from Le Mans cathedral (see H. Kraus, *The Living Theatre of Medieval Art*, London 1967, pp. 160–1). Photo: Archives photographiques

125 Wolfram and tolerance, from a MS of *Willehalm* of *c.* 1250–75: Munich: Bayerische Staatsbibliothek, MS Germ. 193, III, f. iv. Photo: Bayerische Staatsbibliothek, Munich

126 St Francis, a Florentine painting (*c.* 1250) now in the Bardi Chapel in Santa Croce, Florence. Photo: Scala

127 Eadmer's handwriting. The opening of the *Historia Novorum* in his autograph MS, Corpus Christi College, Cambridge, MS 452, p. 1 (see R.W. Southern, *St Anselm and his Biographer*, Cambridge 1963, pp. 372 ff., and also pp. 298 ff.). Photo: By permission of the Master and Fellows of Corpus Christi College, Cambridge

128 Terence, a scene from the *Andria* in a mid-twelfth century MS: Oxford, Bodleian Library, MS Auct. F.2.13, f. 28v. Photo: Bodleian Library

129 Tristan, three scenes from a German MS of the first half of the thirteenth century. Munich, Bayerische Staatsbibliothek, MS Germ. 51, f. 90r. Photo: Bayerische Staatsbibliothek, Munich

130 Parzival and Feirefiz, from a German MS of *Parzival*, *c.* 1250: Munich, Bayerische Staatsbibliothek, MS Germ. 19, f. 49v. Photo: Bayerische Staatsbibliothek, Munich

131 Baptism of Feirefiz, from the same *Parzival* MS, *c.* 1250. Ibid. f. 50v. Photo: Bayerische Staatsbibliothek, Munich

132 A drinking song, from the MS of Benedictbeuern of *c.* 1225, the *Carmina Burana*, which contains the lyric on our pp. 190, 192: Munich, Bayerische Staatsbibliothek, MS Lat. 4660, f. 89v. Photo: Bayerische Staatsbibliothek, Munich

The map on p. 193 was drawn by S. Schotten

INDEX

Page numbers in italics refer to illustrations